Praise for *The Intuitive Heart*

"For those who wish a potent, personal transformation, I invite you to open your body, mind, and heart to the wisdom of this marvelous book."

C. Norman Shealy, M.D., Ph.D.
Coauthor of *Sacred Healing*
Founder, Shealy Wellness Center

"*[The Intuitive Heart]* is a gem . . . Particularly useful for solving relationship problems, the book insightfully shows that only love from the intuitive heart can open the higher mind to the inner knowledge of intuition."

Alan Vaughan
Author of *Doorways to Higher Consciousness*

"This book offers a guiding light that can last a lifetime—a heart-centered approach to intuition. This is a book that I have long awaited. It is based on wisdom that is grounded in years of both teaching and intuitive practice. While it focuses on the life of the soul, it is informed by solid scholarship. I highly recommend it."

Jeffrey Mishlove, Ph.D.
President, Intuition Network
Author of *The Roots of Consciousness*
Host of *Thinking Allowed* TV show

"*The Intuitive Heart* is a wonderful 'how-to' guide that will open you up to the wisdom of your intuition. It shows you practical ways to access this guidance and use it to live a full and rewarding life."

A. Robinson
or of *Divine Intuition: Guide to a Life You Love*

D1167019

"The information in this book is enduring and doesn't fade away after one reading or practice session. It is lasting and becomes even more reliable and trusted as you continue with your practice."

Marcia Emery, Ph.D.
Author of *The Intuitive Healer* and
Dr. Marcia Emery's Intuition Workbook

"Henry Reed has written a gentle and compassionate book centered on the heart, yet informed by his years of first-class academic training and research . . . He has worked out a simple six-step program that people have used with consistently reported success."

Stephan A. Schwartz, Ph.D.
Author of *The Secret Vaults of Time* and
The Alexandria Project

The Intuitive Heart

Also by Henry Reed:

Getting Help from Your Dreams
Dream Solutions, Dream Realizations
Mysteries of the Mind
Channeling Your Higher Self

Also by Brenda English

The Sutton McPhee Mystery Series:
Corruption of Faith
Corruption of Power
Corruption of Justice

The Intuitive

Heart

How to Trust Your Intuition for Guidance and Healing

Henry Reed, Ph.D.,
and
Brenda English

ARE PRESS

ASSOCIATION FOR RESEARCH AND ENLIGHTENMENT

A.R.E. Press • Virginia Beach • Virginia

A.R.E. Press
215 67th Street
Virginia Beach, VA 23451-2061

Reed, Henry.
    The intuitive heart : how to trust your intuition for guidance
and healing / Henry Reed and Brenda English.
        p.   cm.
    ISBN 0-87604-474-7
    1. Intuition (Psychology). I. English, Brenda. II. Title.
BF315.5R43   2000
153.4'4—dc21

                                    00-056942

Cover design by Lightbourne

Intuitive Heart design by Veronica Reed

Contents

Foreword

*L*et me use Dr. Henry Reed's magnificent Intuitive Heart discovery process as a way to give you a clue about his book.

The process asks me to draw upon a memory to awaken my intuition. My memory is of walking along the Paradise Island Beach in the Bahamas. I walk toward the calm, blue-green water and stand by the water's edge, watching the small waves that are gently breaking on the shore. They carry with them a bounty of beautiful shells that are deposited at my feet. Some look like castles, pine cones, and even a snail shell or two. As I stand there, I retrieve another memory of a favorite saying from Dr. Jonas Salk : "I wonder what my intuition will toss up to me like gifts from the sea."

As I stand there wondering what gifts from the sea will

be given to me, I think of Henry's impressive book, which you are about to read. The parallel is so striking. As part of your intuition training, you will be retrieving memories, tossed up to you from your infinite sea of consciousness and that will connect you with your intuition, leading you to the perfect guidance. Your connections with others will be deepened, and a broad perspective provided for any career, personal need, or troubling issue, will be retrieved. What a gift! All of this comes from learning how to fish in the waters of your own inner reservoir to retrieve intuitive insights.

How privileged you are to have Dr. Henry Reed, an outstanding researcher and teacher, show you how to cultivate your intuition by honing your storytelling skills. With a story, you are using an example to show and then teach an inspiring lesson to reveal an underlying truth that will trigger a deeper wisdom from the soul.

Let me share a story about Henry and myself that will show you how intuition works for me. In 1991, Henry and I were among the eighty-five attendees in Honolulu at the first annual Global Intuition Network conference. I was one of two individuals being presented an award and had to demonstrate my gifts as a practicing intuitive to the audience. For my presentation, I had planned to have a member of the audience find a resolution to a burning issue by using my intuitive problem-solving technique. In the weeks leading up to this moment, my logical mind occasionally went into overwhelm because my intuitive process, which usually requires privacy for centering, would be so publicly witnessed.

My intuitive mind calmed me and showed me the image of "a dark blue shirt" which was the key to a successful intuitive demonstration. From that image, I knew I had to look for a person in a dark blue shirt. The intuitive process, as you will learn throughout the pages in this book, is all about trust. And I trusted right up until the moment that I asked for a volunteer from the audience. Hands shot up everywhere, and I quickly found my man in the blue shirt—Henry Reed. An enlightening experience resulted as we embraced each other in this adventure of the heart. The wisdom from the intuitive mind, of course, provided the wisest answer.

Notice the lessons in my story as I share this 1991 memory with you. My intuitive mind, embracing the larger picture, gave me the blue shirt image way in advance of my attending this event. I didn't have a verbal description of a person, but simply saw a picture of a blue shirt. Though I didn't understand what the image meant, I felt very comfortable in my body and trusted that I was given a significant key. I also trusted that my intuitive mind could accurately foreshadow a successful outcome just by my connecting with the blue shirt. Otherwise, I would have diminished my intuition by imagining many failure scenarios. I simply counteracted any fear thoughts with my trust. Finally, I had a heart connection with another person and knew that the wisdom coming to us from a higher source would be in the best interest of all concerned.

Here's our connection from my story to your upcoming learning experience. Dr. Reed will show you how to ignite your intuition as you start with a memory and then graduate to images and thoughts. You, too, will learn to trust the wisdom implicit in this memory as you make a heartful connection with another person to retrieve an invaluable insight.

The best-kept secret is finally being exposed! Everyone has intuitive ability. This is not a gift bestowed upon a chosen few. As you go through the pages in this book, keep reminding yourself that you are already intuitive and now have the opportunity to hone this precious inner resource. Henry Reed is a consummate teacher with passion and heart. You could not ask for a better guide to lead you into his Intuitive Heartland. This skill will be perfected as you refine your awareness and listening skills. As Henry points out, by "paying attention to the thoughts, feelings, and images that come to mind, you are learning to tune into your intuition. " As memories surface, you will discover the significant clues they provide for guiding you in your day-to-day activities. Intuitive input for healing a relationship challenge, for example, is given when you receive a memory of the time you answered the door bell to find a delivery person handing you a bunch of balloons. This unexpected gift came from a client thanking you for your advice. You transfer that memory to your wounded relationship situation and realize that sending a gift to this injured friend without waiting for a special occasion will provide just the right healing balm for your strained relationship.

As a teacher and author of books on intuition, I applaud so many of the features in this book. For example, what could be more important than a focus on the breath as a way to initiate the intuitive process? Yet, this is often omitted in other training programs. As we take our shallow breaths for granted, we remain in a limited perspective, which shifts when we deepen the breath and grow into a more expansive space. Another feature I laud is the focus on gratitude. According to the well-known *Course In Miracles*, the prayer of the heart is gratitude. And gratitude, as suggested is so needed to elevate our consciousness. The treasured value of making the heart connection allows us to step away from our own concerns to help another, which also helps us develop empathy.

I so appreciate that Henry is training you to develop your intuitive ability so you can really penetrate to the core of any difficulty and retrieve a larger perspective on the issue in need of healing or understanding. Too often, the aim of an intuitive development class is geared toward developing predictive skills. "Taint necessarily so," says Dr. Reed, who leads you, the reader, into a deeper excursion through the layers of the psyche to find buried treasures that may reflect stuffed grievances, unresolved conflicts, unrealized hopes and wishes, as well as acute pains. This drilling deeply into the psyche is so needed to retrieve the memories that can benefit from the healing.

Any time I teach through my books, classes, and lectures, I always alert my audience to the culprits that distort intuitive input. Coming from the limited ego space, these false pretenders are wishful thinking, fear, and projection. Dr. Reed leads us higher into the heart to connect with the higher emotions that help us make a genuine heart connection, so we may fully open our eyes and appreciate the unlimited possibilities in the situation.

The information you retrieve from this book is enduring and doesn't fade away after one reading or practice session. It is lasting and becomes even more reliable and trusted as you continue to persist with your practice. That reminds me of the old joke: How do you get to Carnegie Hall? The answer? Practice, practice, and practice! Practice this Intuitive Heart technique until you can effortlessly use your intuitive lens to probe any dimly lit situation. You will emerge with a sense of pride that you have taken the responsibility to seek and find the needed clarification.

Marcia Emery, Ph.D.
Author of *The Intuitive Healer* and
Dr. Marcia Emery's Intuition Workbook.

Introduction

*O*nce, I thought that intuition was something that some people were graced with at birth—and which the rest of us just have to struggle to acquire. I was convinced that I was one of those persons who had to struggle to "get" it. I had this viewpoint despite the fact that a psychic thread runs in my family. But perhaps because I wasn't like the psychic performers I saw in the media, I discounted my own innate ability.

Then I awakened to the fact that intuition is a natural gift born in everyone. Some people seem more naturally at ease with it than others, but everyone has the ability to be wonderfully intuitive. However, even when I recognized my own intuitive ability, I still treated it like a product. It was something you "had," and you could put it to use whenever you needed it, just like a handy tool in your toolbox.

Then I had another awakening. Intuition is not something you have, but is a way of being. The more you allow your intuition to open, the more you change, and your life changes profoundly with you. You experience a deeper wisdom about yourself, about life, and about living your life according to the highest principles. Your heart opens. Intuition brings out the authentic self.

Along the path of these awakenings, I was drawn to the warm, witty, and wise work of Henry Reed.

I remember clearly what I was thinking as I sat in the audience of one particular workshop. Henry had just explained how we were going to do an intuition exercise, which involved tapping into our memories. I was intrigued, but skeptical. It seemed radically different from other exercises I'd learned.

"I don't see how this can work," I thought, "at least for me." By the end of the exercise, I was astonished, not only by my results, but also by the unique process Henry had developed for allowing intuition to blossom. I was excited, because Henry was teaching what I was already experiencing: that intuition is not just a gift or ability, but a way of life.

Many books on intuition teach techniques. A few teach how to make intuition a natural part of your lifestyle. Even fewer show how intuition becomes in itself a path of love through life. All of these gifts—techniques, lifestyle, and path—are delivered in Henry's book, *The Intuitive Heart*, coauthored by Brenda English.

Three terms come to mind that describe Henry's work. One is "innovative." You can count on Henry to be at the frontiers of creativity and change. A second term is "effective." The innovative techniques and approaches Henry develops in his teaching are always effective. A third term is "loving." Henry's work is innovative and effective because he approaches it, and life, from a point of love.

A good teacher is someone who enables you to discover for yourself what you are capable of achieving. A good teacher is someone who helps you bring out your best. In *The Intuitive Heart*, Henry invites you to step onto the path of love and discover what your intuition is and how it speaks to you. From the moment you begin, you are fully engaged in the process, gently circling the labyrinth of yourself to your own deep center. You discover that intuition is much more than obtaining answers to questions about what to do. It concerns becoming one with everything around you—with all life. This is truly being "in the flow." When we are in the flow, we experience a wonderful fullness of life. Not only do we improve our own lives, we are able to help others, too, and from a point of love, empathy, and compassion. We bring out our best.

One of the hardest hurdles facing people in intuition is trusting what they get. It's easy to second-guess and wonder if your inner guidance is intuition or imagination. For a number of years, I gave psychic readings—or "intuitive consultations," as many people call them now. First, I did them informally for friends and then professionally for clients. I don't think I ever gave a single reading in which the client did not already know the answers to the questions he or she brought to the session, even if they professed that they didn't. They sought readings because they didn't trust what they already knew from their own intuitive wisdom, or perhaps they weren't ready to acknowledge what they already knew. Sometimes they wanted an outside authority to tell them what to do. They didn't know how to retrieve their own wisdom.

Like Henry, I'd much rather see people realize and

trust their own intuition. Your Higher Self truly knows what is in your best interests and will guide you accordingly. You have everything within you to obtain the guidance you need.

What I especially like about *The Intuitive Heart* is how easily Henry's process moves you into trust and confidence. Your own wisdom, accumulated from your life experiences, is stored in memories. Henry shows you how to work with your memories to make powerful connections to your own wisdom. Everything is drawn from within.

Following *The Intuitive Heart* will help you with much more than decisions—it will enhance your ability to love and be close to others. As we go through life, we are called to higher and higher ideals. I call this the "Path of Beauty, Virtue, and Truth."

Beauty is a dimension of heaven that we experience when we show respect for all others and all life, and also when we see the beauty in another soul. *The Intuitive Heart* will show you Beauty.

Virtue is right living, which is not a monk's life, but the life that unfolds when we open to love: We are where we need to be, and we do what we are meant to do. *The Intuitive Heart* will take you there.

Truth is undefinable, something that we intuit and understand in a mystical way. Truth concerns the Great Mystery, and we all must discover it for ourselves. *The Intuitive Heart* will open you to Truth.

Enjoy the journey!

Rosemary Ellen Guiley
Author of *Breakthrough Intuition* and
Dreamwork for the Soul

1

The Heart Has a Natural Feel for Intuition

"I shall light a candle of understanding in thy heart, which shall not be put out."   Apocrypha, II Esdras 14:25

*L*isa had an important decision to make. She could stay in her current job or accept the offer of a former co-worker who was starting a new company. Lisa believed her current job was secure, and she made a good salary. While her friend's new company had a lot of potential, it also presented some large question marks. When Lisa asked the advice of her other friends, they all told her she would be crazy, in a downsizing business climate, to give up a secure job for the unknown.

But Lisa recently had become concerned with

how her work life fit into the rest of her life, with the effects it had on her, on how she viewed herself, and how she viewed those around her. In her quiet moments, she felt more and more drawn to the idea of a job such as the one being offered her, and so she finally accepted her friend's invitation.

Six months later, the entire section where Lisa previously had worked was eliminated by her former employer. Meanwhile, the new company Lisa had joined was growing daily.

"I listened to my intuition," Lisa explained, "my new job has proven to be a much better fit, psychologically and spiritually, as well as careerwise. I've learned I always regret it when I don't listen to the voice of my intuition."

John, too, had a major decision to make. While Lisa's choice involved her career, John found himself on the horns of a much more personal dilemma. At 38, he was still a bachelor. He had never married because Lana, the one woman he felt he had loved and whom he had dated in college, had married John's best friend, Bill, instead. Now, fifteen years later, Lana had divorced Bill and had come to John on the rebound, saying she should have married him instead.

Elated that his heart's desire was coming true, John ignored the inner voice that warned him to go slowly, to be cautious. He married Lana within two months of her reappearance in his life. Things went rapidly downhill, however, and within months, John found himself in divorce court after learning that Lisa already had begun an affair with a third man.

"I should have listened to that little voice that was

nagging at me, telling me something was wrong with this picture," John said later, nursing his twice-broken heart. "I won't make that mistake again."

Chances are these two stories sound familiar. You may have had, as most of us have, both kinds of experiences, those times when you followed what you may have called a hunch and things worked out, as well as other times when you didn't listen to your inner voice, much to your later regret.

These days, the idea of turning to your intuition for guidance has even become trendy. There is a growing interest in intuition, not just in the self-help section of the bookstores, but also in corporations and boardrooms. The International Institute of Management in Geneva, Switzerland, for example, concluded after a major investigation that intuition will be the most important management resource of the next decade. Why?

The answer is a combination of the information explosion and the rapidly increasing pace of changes in that information. There will be, in fact may already be, too much information to process through conventional analytical means. Even if you have time to analyze the information, by the time you've completed the analysis, the information will have changed. How can you keep your eye on the ball when you can't even find the ball? The management institute's answer? Intuition.

You also might be interested in knowing what role the institute sees for intuition. First, these experts say, intuition is useful in getting a vision of where you want to go, in deciding which "mountain" is worth climbing. Second, intuition is useful in deciding the best place to start. Finally, intuition comes in handy along the way, at each crossroad where you have to make a decision.

Many Nobel-winning scientists apparently agree with

the management institute. When they were interviewed after receiving the coveted prize, most of the winning scientists agreed that they used intuition in their work. The most common use was to decide which problem would be most interesting to study and which approach to the problem would yield the best results.

Could the intuition illustrated in these management and science examples apply as well to you and me in our everyday lives? In this journey called life, we all have to make decisions about where we want to go and how we are going to get there. When we come up against obstacles or have important decisions to make, how are we going to proceed, particularly when we can't see the future or access all the relevant information? Such major crossroads in our lives would seem to be excellent opportunities for using intuition.

Ever Regret Not Following a Hunch?

"My eyes deceive me, but my heart cannot."   Heinrich Lersch

The truth is that, in spite of all the increased interest in intuition and in spite of those times when our intuition has steered us right, most of us still hesitate to follow something that we can't pin down to a set of facts or rules. And we often regret it later.

Just about everyone understands what a hunch is. It's that feeling that seemingly comes from somewhere inside and that says you should or should not do something. Regret over not following a hunch is almost a universal experience. Because it is so common, it's a subject in which nearly everyone is interested, and I have found it to be a useful way of introducing the broader subject of intuition. Many people have found that it was their regret over not following a hunch that proved to be their initiation into a greater respect for their intuition. We can learn a lot from those experiences.

I've met a surprising number of people who, like John, have stories about getting a strong hunch not to go through with a wedding, for instance. But they got married anyway, and later, they regretted not having called off the wedding. Why did they go ahead and get married? It was too late to stop it, they explain. Or there were too many plans made, too many people involved. And, they ask, what could they have said to other people, to their fiance? Surely, one can't just say, "Well, I have this gut feeling that I shouldn't do this."

Their stories provide good examples of some of the reasons why we often don't trust our intuition. It's difficult to explain to others. We aren't sure if we're getting it right, and there's no way to check our sources. Very often there is already much invested in going against intuition's promptings. Intuition can be difficult to substantiate, at least until after the fact, thus making it hard to defend intuition to others.

When I ask people why they often don't trust their intuition, they usually cite similar reasons. Whether their decisions involved relationships, career changes, important purchases or investments, or some other type of concern, or whether their answer is that it was inconvenient, that it went against what others believed, or that they didn't want to believe in intuition themselves, for many people, not following a hunch usually comes down to not feeling able to trust one's inner self in the absence of outside support. So, what is it that makes intuition so difficult to trust?

Intuition Is An Inner Experience

"One of the hardest things in life is having words in your heart that
you can't utter."   James Earl Jones

To an outside observer, intuition seems to be an intangible, internal, private event. There's nothing you can
offer to enable others to share your intuition. There's
nothing you can point to outside yourself to justify or
explain your intuition.

These negatives show up even in defining intuition.
People often use negatives in describing what intuition
is. They will say that intuition is knowing without knowing how you know. Or that it is knowing something without any reason for knowing it. Or perhaps, that it's
knowing without using any outside information. All
these definitions of intuition involve negatives. They
emphasize what intuition lacks. They focus on the mysterious quality of intuition, on how little we know about
it and thus, on how little we feel we can trust it.

When we approach intuition in this way, we are especially unable to answer the logical question: How do we
know? The lack of a concrete, easily identifiable answer
to the question of how intuition works has proven to be
a liability for intuition's reputation. In our scientific,
technological society, intuition has had little public status. If you can't show it to someone else, produce it on
demand, ensure reproducible results, or pinpoint exactly where the information comes from, then it isn't real
or valid.

To make matters worse, intuition often presents its
messages in personal symbols and inner feelings that
lack the status of outward signs on whose meaning we
all can agree. While even successful businessmen and
scientists may use intuition, they often keep that fact to

themselves. Intuition remains a private matter and thus doesn't benefit from the kinds of education and development that sharing would encourage. This private aspect of intuition has made it difficult for it to achieve any respectable stature in our society.

The result is that many of us learn not to trust our intuition. When we get an intuition, we have no training for how to deal with it. Alone with our intuition, we have nothing at which we can point to back it up. There are no facts to show, no logic for others to follow, just an inner feeling. So we are apt to question its validity, to second-guess it with logic or contrary information. Only later, when we come to regret not listening to our intuition, do we despair over this unfortunate state of affairs, this feeling that we don't know how to trust intuition's messages. Isn't there a better way to learn to respect intuition, we wonder, than through regret over having ignored it?

A Possible Solution to the Trust Problem

"Go to your bosom, Knock there, and ask your heart what it doth know ... " William Shakespeare, *Measure for Measure*

I think I have found a way that each of us can use to demonstrate to our own satisfaction that intuition is real, that it works, and that we *can* trust it.

First, let's do something different. Let's define intuition in a positive, straightforward manner. Let's say simply that intuition means knowing from within. It is an inner knowing. Period. And although it is knowing from within, I think there are ways we can share this inner knowing with others in such a way that we can learn more about intuition. There's a way we can share with others the experience of learning about how intuition operates and what it has to offer.

I have made an important discovery about intuition that will be very helpful to you. In fact, there is a way you can learn to recognize and trust your intuition. It took me twenty-plus years of research into dreams, creativity, and expanded consciousness to make this discovery. When you realize what it is, you may say, "I already knew that!" If so, you'll receive some confirmation of your own natural intuition. On the other hand, if you aren't familiar with your intuition, you'll learn something new, as I have, something that, with some time and practice, you can make a practical part of your life. In either case, I believe that what I've discovered is important enough to write this book in order to make the idea public and explicit.

My discovery is that *love and caring are a natural source of intuition. Intuition is most effective when it comes from caring, from a sincere wish to make a heart connection, either with your own inner self or with another.* I call my discovery **the Intuitive Heart**.

People always have known, at an intuitive level, that the heart is naturally intuitive. Just look at the English language. We regularly use phrases such as knowing something in our hearts, feeling that someone or something touched our hearts, our hearts being joined, finding it in our hearts to do one thing or another, speaking from the heart. The list of examples goes on and on. What all these phrases illustrate is that we already know the truth: that the heart holds the key to intuition.

The foundation of my discovery of the Intuitive Heart is that caring about someone creates a natural bridge of intuitive understanding of that person. We sometimes say that we take someone into our hearts. This common phrase means that we come to have empathy and compassion for that other person. Those two qualities, empathy and compassion, come together as a natural intuitive team. Compassion and caring create a means of understanding by helping us empathize in a particularly sensitive and imaginative way.

Intuition also has an important connection with love, whether it is love for a person, a situation, or even a subject in which we are interested. Intuition comes about as a result of having embraced that person, situation or subject with love. Love has its own gift of intelligence. As you will see, when the foundation is love, intuition has the potential to improve our lives in varied and significant ways.

When we care enough to offer something of ourselves, our intuition guides our giving. Many of us are naturally intuitive when we care about someone or something outside ourselves. It is the commonality of this type of other-directed intuitive experience that tells me I have discovered something important. People often believe that they can be intuitive some of the time, especially when they aren't thinking about it, when it happens naturally. It is those natural, spontaneous moments of intuition that tell me the importance of my insight into the heart's role in intuition.

Take Susan's experience, for example:

When Susan and Ruth met for lunch, Ruth didn't seem her usual cheerful self. Susan didn't want to pry, but she did want to help. To take Ruth's mind off whatever was bothering her, Susan asked for Ruth's advice. Susan explained that she was having a problem with Kelly, a co-worker who took Susan's every question or difference of opinion as a personal attack. As she described the situation to Ruth, Susan realized, to her embarrassment, that she was contributing to her own problem because she nearly always began her comments to Kelly with phrases such as "That won't work because . . . "

"No wonder she gets angry," Susan said, in sudden understanding. "I'm always looking for what's wrong with her ideas, and I'm never seeing what's good about them."

At that, Ruth immediately brightened and said, "Oh Susan, how interesting that you should say that! It's exactly what I needed to hear."

Ruth explained that she had been worried and distracted because she and her fourteen-year-old son were constantly at odds.

"What you just said made me realize that I do the same thing to him," Ruth said. "In my frustration with him, I've gotten into a bad habit of always talking about what's wrong with his behavior. I think I should start looking instead for what's right with it."

In her desire to take Ruth's mind off her troubles, Susan had searched her mind for something to say. She had grabbed at the first thing that came up, just to get the conversation going in another direction. Yet her subject matter and her insight into her own behavior had touched Ruth in a special way. In some manner outside Susan's conscious intentions, she had reached inside herself and come up with exactly the right story. Not only had it given Susan insight into her own problem, but it also had shown Ruth a possible solution to what was bothering her. How was it that Susan knew the right thing to say, even though she didn't know what Ruth's concern was, didn't know she was saying the right thing? She was being intuitive. In fact, she was being intuitive without even knowing it, without intending to.

We all can appreciate Susan's story. Without realizing it, she was being intuitive as a natural outgrowth of her empathy for Ruth. What if we try to apply Susan's story to being intuitive ourselves? Most of us find that if we focus on it, if we try intentionally to be intuitive, we doubt our ability. We suspect that we will get in our own way, that we will just be making it up or guessing, or that trying too hard will wreck it. But I have found that *by using a heart-centered approach, people easily can be intentionally intuitive.*

I'll tell you more about this approach as we go along but, briefly, this heart-centered approach is based on where you physically focus your attention when you look for an intuition. In fact, when many people look for inner guidance and for connections with those around them, they seem to focus naturally and instinctively on the chest area—on the heart. If you search for wisdom there, within your own heart, you will find it.

Can I Trust My Heart?

"I follow my heart for I can trust it."
J.C. Friederich von Schiller, *Wallerstein's Tod*

Learning to access your intuition brings up the issue of trust. How can you learn to trust your intuition? How can you learn to trust your inner knowing, trust yourself? If, when you look to your intuition for an answer, you often doubt that you are getting pure intuition uncontaminated by your hopes and fears, how can you know that you are getting the best guidance possible?

Once again, working with intuition from a heart-centered perspective provides a very useful answer to the problem of trust. Integrity and honesty are very important in making intuition reliable. And what better way to achieve these qualities than through love, which the heart so intelligently provides? The intuitive heart asks, in love, what is the best for all concerned. It is willing to listen to the higher guidance of love and to the direction that love might suggest. *Love gives your intuition the integrity it needs to become trustworthy.*

You may be skeptical. For many of us, love carries connotations that have more to do with romance than with intuition. But I have some things to share with you that will change your mind.

In the "research laboratory" I use today—seminars, teaching college classes, counseling sessions, and training programs in office settings—I have seen repeated demonstrations of heart-centered intuition producing uncanny connections, even between people who are strangers to each other, and even in people who never have thought of themselves as psychic, telepathic, or intuitive, or as anything more than just average people. My observations demonstrate clearly that intuition is available to all of us. It is a normal, natural ability that we all have and that we all can access—when we experience it from the heart.

By teaching you a very specific method for receiving intuitive guidance, I will show you how you can come to trust your intuition, how you can access it reliably and get meaningful results that can improve your ability to make decisions in your life, to make connections with those around you, and to know that your intuitions are valid. The methods I will show you, which are based directly on my years of research, can help awaken your intuitive abilities, can help you form a meaningful relationship with those abilities. You'll learn to use your intuition as a valuable guide. You'll learn to trust your Intuitive Heart.

Another advantage to the heart-centered approach is that intuition is not simply the ability to guess what lottery number a computer will create. It is about much more than facts; it also includes values, possibilities, relationships. Intuition is a dimension of emotional intelligence that gives you insights into people, into their potential. As emotional intelligence, it also helps you see your relationships with people, with unseen dimensions, and with future possibilities. So intuition provides creative perspectives on people and situations. At its best, it provides wisdom and guidance. Moreover, heart-centered intuition is not simply a once-in-a-while thing, a "flash" of intuition. It is a continually-operative connection with the world around you, guiding you in your affairs as you "feel" your way into situations. It is readily available to speak directly to you when you need it.

By approaching intuition from the heart, you can come to experience it, recognize it, and, above all, trust it. The Intuitive Heart method is one that you can use to see your own intuitive abilities at work. All that is required is to put aside your mistrust for a short time and to take a chance on opening yourself to the universal wisdom that is within you. I think what you find will surprise and, perhaps, astonish you with the wisdom of your own Intuitive Heart.

It all seems so obvious to me now, when I put it this way, but it wasn't obvious when I began my research into intuition. As you will see, it took some time to recognize what I had found and then to develop specific ways to translate that knowledge into a practical method for accessing the Intuitive Heart. The road to my discovery of the Intuitive Heart began in the university laboratory. It wasn't a direct road by any means, but by taking a quick look at the path I followed to the Intuitive Heart, I think you will understand better how natural a part of all of us our Intuitive Hearts really are.

2

Discovering Your Intuitive Heart

"A good heart is better than all the heads in the world."
Bulwer-Lytton, *The Disowned*

The setting for the story I want to tell you was a "dream circle" at a recent seminar I was giving on developing intuition. Each person in the circle had agreed to have a dream about the unknown concern of a designated "target person" in the group, and now the group was hearing those dreams from the night before.

One person dreamed of a school bus driven over a cliff on the side of a beautiful mountain. Another dreamed of a broken-down car that she worried would be expensive to repair, especially when she had just quit her job to pursue a new career. A third dreamed of orange highway caution cones laid out on a driving school roadway. Then, she saw the cones fitted inside each other, where they began to turn together like a car's transmission. The fourth dreamed of a teacher who realized the school bus she was waiting for didn't come to the elevated platform where she stood with her students. Instead, she had to come down to the street to catch the bus. There, a passerby told her that the new wing she wanted for the school was possible but that she would have to put some money up front first.

The people in the circle, all strangers to each other, were volunteers in an experiment. They all had been asked to dream for Beverly. All they knew about Beverly was that she had a pressing personal concern or problem. The catch was that the dreamers weren't told in advance what that concern was. Yet, their task was to have a dream that would help Beverly resolve her issue. On their return to the group the next day, they all came in shaking their heads, feeling that their individual dreams might have some personal meaning for themselves, but convinced that they had failed to dream anything remotely related to Beverly.

As the dreamers shared their dreams, however, some common patterns soon emerged. They began to suspect that their dreams were onto something. There were many references to cars being directed in some way, as if something had gone wrong and was trying to be put right. There were many scenarios concerning the theme of worrying about money. There also were several references to school and instruction.

Asked to speculate on what the target person's concern might be and its possible resolution, the group decided that it might involve decisions about a life track or career that had gone wrong somehow and that needed to be redirected. There seemed to be a definite message that an investment of time, money, and education would be required. Schools certainly seemed to be involved.

Once Beverly heard all the group's dreams and their thoughts about the meanings, it was her turn to speak. She explained her problem. She was a former teacher who had left the stress of teaching years before to take an office job. She now realized her mistake and wanted to return to teaching, only to be thwarted by her lack of current credentials and her inability to decide what teaching direction to take.

Suddenly, each of the dreams made amazing sense. A career had gone off track and broken down. A heart wanted to teach again but knew it would have to get down to basics (the street level) of retraining and credentialing to do so. There were concerns about the money Beverly would have to invest in herself at a time when she was unemployed. There was a message that the career could go forward only when the parts fit together.

After much discussion, Beverly left the session elated, feeling that the dreams had gotten to the heart of her dilemma and had pointed her in a productive new direction.

A Circle of Intuitive Dreamers Brings Enlightenment

"Hearts may agree though heads differ."
                                      Thomas Fuller, *Gnomologia*

While you might expect the uncanny accuracy of the dream symbols in this example to be a rare occurrence, in fact, such accuracy is not at all unusual in my experience. It happens almost all the time whenever this experiment is attempted, either by me or by someone else. I named this experiment in group dreaming the Dream Helper Ceremony. I call it a ceremony because it has the personal drama of something special and set apart from ordinary life, and because it is something that has a special purpose.

I have used the Dream Helper Ceremony to research and make important discoveries about people and their dreams. I do not conduct it in a sterile laboratory, but at retreat centers and seminar locations all over the world. I have helped people conduct it in their homes with family and friends. I have trained others to use it as a teaching tool for classes in churches and community colleges. Over and over, at these workshops and dreamwork groups, I, and many others who have conducted the Dream Helper Ceremony, see this kind of scenario repeated. Strangers come together with the commitment to help another and, without even knowing the question, are able to find within themselves a dream that carries a very pertinent message.

In hindsight, it would seem obvious that intuition must be at work in such dreams. But hindsight follows a much straighter line than the one I followed to the Dream Helper Ceremony. It was a major waystation in my journey to finding the idea of the Intuitive Heart. The journey began while I was in training as a psychologist.

My background is in traditional psychology research. My credentials include a Ph.D., with honors, from UCLA; an assistant professorship at Princeton University; and a sabbatical of research at the C.G. Jung Sleep and Dream Laboratory in Zurich, Switzerland. My early research during those years, into the mechanics of memory, made me realize that, like many people, I didn't remember my dreams. I worked hard to learn how to remember them and learned how I might help others do so also. This led me to research how people remember dreams and, eventually, into a study of how to have dreams that were worth remembering.

I wanted to develop a technique that people could use

to dream about a particular question for which they needed guidance or inspiration. But I was not comfortable that the environment of the traditional university sleep laboratory would be conducive to the type of inspirational dreams I was hoping people would have.

At a timely juncture in my explorations, I received an invitation to be a research consultant to the Edgar Cayce Foundation in Virginia Beach, Virginia, and to help them design a research program for the foundation's membership organization, the Association for Research and Enlightenment, Inc. (A.R.E.®) The research design needed to be consistent with the spiritual ideals and vision for research set out by Edgar Cayce. Cayce, who died in 1945, was one of the most well-known and well-documented psychics in history. His vision of research into areas of human development was quite idealistic. Rather than an artificial environment in which some people were guinea pigs and tested by others, Cayce envisioned research that would revolve around people cooperating, working together in a mutually informed manner, to explore ways of being truly helpful to one another, in order to bring about greater understanding and personal development for all.

In this consulting work, I also had the opportunity to conduct dream research at the A.R.E.'s summer camp for young people. On the basis of a personal dream involving a tent, my own happy memories of camping as a Boy Scout, and my knowledge of inspirational ceremonies used by groups around the world, I developed the idea of a "dream tent" as a special sanctuary in which a youngster would sleep when seeking dream guidance.

The research with the dream tent was successful. You can read the details in my book, *Getting Help from Your Dreams*, but the procedure basically went like this:

After a day of mental and spiritual preparation, much

like the preparation of Native Americans for some of their visionary ceremonies, the seeker would spend the night in the dream tent with the intent of having a special dream—which usually came. As one religious scholar who wrote about my research on this "dream incubation" concluded, it proved that the spiritual dreams associated with biblical stories of the past are still possible today. That was the success of the research: It demonstrated the possibility of *spiritual* dreaming.

But something else, something unexpected, happened as well. As the camp session progressed and the other campers also told me their dreams, I discovered that someone else in camp often would have a dream connected to the person sleeping in the tent. While the connection usually was not obvious to the outside dreamer, it was apparent to me because I was aware of the issue the person in the tent was trying to resolve. I called these "bystander" dreams because it seemed as if the outside dreamers were participating vicariously in the dream tent experience, as if they were trying to help the person sleeping there. But how could that happen?

I soon realized that the dream tent was in a very public part of the camp. The dream seeker spent the day alone at the tent site, thinking and meditating, but very much in view of the other campers. I realized, too, that the atmosphere of the whole camp, one of cooperation, spiritual support, and affirmation based on Edgar Cayce's philosophy, probably instilled in the campers a desire to support the person who was seeking a dream for guidance. Was I witnessing a special sort of dream telepathy or ESP, I wondered? If so, could I find a way to have such dream ESP operate intentionally?

The dream tent experiment was not designed to investigate ESP, however, and I needed a different experimental design. The search for the right design led me back to another dream of mine, one I had when I first began consulting with the Edgar Cayce Foundation on the problem of bringing idealism to its research methodology.

In my dream, a group of people gathered to search for enlightenment. In the dark, we bumped into each other in great confusion. Then we were inspired to begin dancing in a circle. Each person in the dance met and greeted each other person as they circulated in the round. Suddenly, a gushing fountain of sparks shot up in the middle of the circle, illuminating our space and enabling us to see. We realized that our search for enlightenment had been achieved by the circle dance.

My original interpretation was that this circle dancing reflected the cooperative spirit of the research method for which we had been searching. Later, as I thought about the bystander dreams at the A.R.E. camp, the circle dance dream focused my thinking on the idea of having many dreamers gathered around one central purpose. It occurred to me that I could harness the power of bystander dreaming by putting the person who was seeking guidance at the center of a circle of dreamers who had agreed to dream for this person.

Is My Dream Just for You, or Is It for Me, Too?

"The same heart beats in every human breast."
Matthew Arnold, *The Buried Life*

I tried the dream circle idea, and it succeeded far beyond my expectations. In fact, it worked great! In the story that opened this chapter, you saw it at work.

What I usually find, after listening to the group's "dreamstorming" and the target person's disclosure of the concern, is that everyone is surprised at the number of connections between the dreams and the target person's situation. The animated discussion that usually follows shows that a collection of strangers has been transformed into a circle of healing intimates.

In the Dream Helper Ceremony, I have seen repeatedly that people clearly can link up with another person's undisclosed problem. A group of people can produce a set of dreams that can accurately identify, insightfully diagnose, and creatively prescribe a treatment for this undisclosed problem. In the more than twenty years since I first developed the Dream Helper Ceremony, it has been conducted countless times, by myself and by many other people, with similar surprising and helpful results. At the very least, it is probably one of our best ways of showing people that dreams have value. But it also led me to something much more.

At this point, you may be thinking to yourself that the connections the dreamers find are generalities that could fit anyone's situation, that it's possible to see connections just about anywhere. I have asked myself the same thing. But let me give you another example of the kinds of experiences which showed me that something much more than nonspecific generalities is at work here.

A gathering of senior citizens at an Elderhostel was large enough that I formed two groups of dream helpers. Each group had its own target person on whom to focus the dreaming. The next morning, each group processed the dreams for their respective target person. The two groups came up with very different dream patterns, yet each group was right on the money for its target person and very helpful.

The first group decided the target person's problem involved a health concern, because of the repeated references to the color white, and to nurses, doctors, and hospitals. There was a sense of frustration in the dreams.

The group decided that the dreams were pointing to a need for a change, to change hospitals, treatments, or remedies.

The second group decided that its target person's problem was a family affair, because of the number of references to the dreamers' own families. They decided that the dream patterns pointed to some kind of argument or dispute, a battle of wills. They surmised from the constructive elements in the dreams that the best solution was to do nothing, to let things be, and let the solution work itself out by itself.

So the first group said, "Make a change!" The second group said, "Leave it alone!" The two groups were headed in opposite directions. As it turned out, this difference was completely appropriate.

The target person in the first group was a woman whose concern involved caring for her ailing husband. Although the couple had been with the same family doctor for years, ever since the doctor had joined an HMO, things had not gone well. They didn't like the hospital. They wanted to leave, but didn't want to disappoint the doctor. The woman received from the group's dreams the support she needed to make that necessary, but painful, change.

In the second group, the target person was a man whose question concerned his grandchildren. His wife and daughter-in-law had gotten into an argument a couple of years before. Since then, the grandchildren had not been allowed to visit the grandparents. The grandparents had tried everything to resolve the problem, and even had consulted a lawyer about their legal rights to have access to their grandchildren. The group's dreams helped the man and his wife accept the fact they had to just let go for a while.

So here we had two groups of people, strangers to one

another, dreaming on the same night, in the same hotel, coming up with distinctly different patterns of dreams and forming diametrically opposite conclusions. Each group's offering to its target person, however, was perfectly tailored and fit an important and useful personal need.

Is the Dream Helper Ceremony showing us some kind of dream telepathy? Maybe the dreamers are "reading the mind" of the target person. Perhaps, but there's more to it than that. The dream patterns often can pinpoint the underlying cause of the target person's problem. Is some kind of clairvoyance involved, with the dreamers somehow tapping into facts unavailable to the target person? Again, it's possible, but there's still more to it than that. The helpful suggestions the groups find in the dream patterns reflect something beyond any ordinary psychic ability, perhaps some kind of uncanny wisdom. The healing power of the groups' dreams, to help people through major life transitions, suggests a holistic phenomenon that is truly transpersonal (meaning something that operates on or has significance beyond the personal level).

In the Dream Helper Ceremony, two levels of communication are happening simultaneously. The dreams make personal statements about the dreamer as a way of offering insights for the target person. My dream is "about" me, but it is "for" you, not just about what I have learned, or need to learn, about a personal situation, but a personal situation that also relates to the concern with which you are wrestling.

You can see this type of "in my experience" form of advice being given in the case of Beverly, the former school teacher who wanted to return to her abandoned career. The person who dreamed of the school bus going over the cliff of a beautiful mountain realized his dream was showing him how a direction that had appeared to be beautiful and right really had been a wrong turn. In his own life, he said, he was losing track of what he really cared about—his children—by focusing too much on externals. The dream's message to him was that he needed to invest more time with his children rather than simply trying to earn more money for their welfare. For Beverly, the message was that her decision to quit teaching, a decision that had seemed more profitable at the time, had taken her life in the wrong direction.

The person who dreamed of the broken-down car realized that she would have to make some temporary sacrifices to keep her car—and her new career—going, but that without them, she was going nowhere. For Beverly, the dream carried the message that the career "car" that she had thought would take her to a good place had broken down and that she was going to have to spend some time and money to repair it before it could take her to the place she only now realized she really needed to be.

The person who dreamed of the highway cones turning like a transmission only when they were fitted together saw her dream's relevance to a career change she recently had made, one that had taken a transition of several years to put together. Only now, when she had fitted all the "cones" together, was her life working in the way she always had hoped. Beverly, too, saw the dream's similar meaning for her. She had been turned down in her efforts to go back into teaching right away, after several years away from it. Not until she fitted together the "cones" of new training, new credentials, and a new direction for her desire to teach would her life and career begin to work smoothly.

The person who dreamed of the teacher waiting for the bus was reminded of one of her teachers who always taught that you couldn't just wish for things, but had to get down to the "street level" and make it happen. She had been wishing to expand her own life by trying out for a new position at work and realized she had been just waiting for it to come to her. Instead, she saw she needed to go find out where the opportunity was and go after it. Beverly, too, saw that it was time for her to commit herself to the career shift and make it happen. She had no trouble understanding the message that the "addition to the school" that she wanted to build could happen, but that she would have to put some money up front first.

When we give advice by saying "in my experience," we are using our own lives as a teaching tool for the other person's problem. This same process was at work in the circle's dreams for Beverly. When these people interpreted their dreams for what the dreams meant to them personally, they realized that they were seeing Beverly's situation from within the perspective of themselves. Without knowing what Beverly's concern was, they had empathized with her by finding within their own lives something comparable to what they intuited was happening with Beverly. The help they offered was homegrown, cultivated from their own experience. You soon will see how your personal experiences also play a key role in learning to use and rely on your Intuitive Heart.

Can I Find You In My Heart?

"He fashioneth their hearts alike."   Psalms 33:15

How did the dream helpers achieve this amazing feat of compassionate knowledge? How did groups of strangers, many of whom rarely remember their dreams, let alone use them for constructive purposes, manage to come up with such dream wisdom? It was obvious to me that there was something more than mere ESP going on here, and I continued my search for the key to explain what I saw happening.

A key insight occurred for me, spontaneously and quite by surprise, in the summer of 1980. I was giving the keynote address to the Association for the Study of Dreams, an international conference that was being held at the historic campus of the University of Virginia in Charlottesville. I was talking about the history of research into intentional dreaming and influencing dream content. I outlined the often quite elaborate but only moderately successful attempts that dream lab researchers have made to control the dreams of laboratory subjects. Researchers have used hypnosis, suggestion, and sensory bombardment, among other methods, to try to control a dreamer's dream. I explained that, in my work with the Dream Helper Ceremony, by contrast, I used no such methods.

Right in the middle of my comments to the association, however, I had one of those jolting shifts of consciousness and insight that opens brand new doors. It suddenly occurred to me that, in all my years of doing the dream circles, I never had given the dreamers or target persons any instructions on how to do what I was asking them to do. In fact, not one person had ever even asked me how they were supposed to dream *for* someone else, let alone to dream about someone's undisclosed problem. I suddenly understood that the people in my experiments were completing their task *intuitively.* They didn't ask me how to do it, because they were already doing it, through unconscious, instinctive intuition, without even knowing how they did it.

What the dreamers were doing, I realized, was using some unknown form of intuitive communication. Somehow, they were recognizing something about the person's concern because of something similar within themselves. In other words, they were finding the other person within themselves, within their own experience. They were intuitively reaching out with compassion, as if to say, "I can identify with how it must feel for you because of something I myself have experienced." I call this process intuitive because it fits perfectly with our simple definition of intuition: knowing from within. They came to know the other person's problem from within themselves. They took that person into their heart and knew them there. It was quite a revelation for me!

The Heart's Intuition Is Subjective

"Here the heart
May give a lesson to the head,
And learning wiser grow without his books."

William Cowper, *The Task*

The dreamers were being granted insight into the living situation of another person. Yet this insight came in a special way. Their intuitions were expressed subjectively. The dreams used personal, not objective, terms, expressing their truths in personal symbols and feelings.

The dreamers did not say to the target person, "Oh, I know about you. Your problem is such and such, and you should do thus and so." Instead, the dreamers' insights were that "I'm being reminded of the time when I had a similar problem. Here's what I've learned and how I'm coping, and maybe that will be helpful for this other person."

It all became clear for me. I could *see* intuition at work. Out of a spirit of wishing to be helpful, of generosity and caring, of giving of one's self, the dreamers were making, inwardly and intuitively, an outward connection with the target person's problem, even without consciously knowing what the problem was. Because it came from within, the connection was expressed in the dreamers' own subjective, symbolic terms that also matched up with the outward situation. What the dreamers were doing was making a connection via what I since have come to call the Intuitive Heart.

To describe the process in the Intuitive Heart's language, I would say that the dream helpers reached out with their hearts. They made a heart-to-heart connection with the target person. They took the target person into their own hearts and experienced the person from within themselves. They searched their hearts for wisdom. Their dreams expressed their hearts' truths.

But then, I wondered, are dreams required in order to make such connections? The answer, I learned as I continued my research, is no. In fact, it is possible to tap intuition directly. The keys to doing so are compassion and the subjective connection.

As I used the Dream Helper Ceremony with more and more groups, I began to hear from participants that sometimes insights came to them well ahead of their dreams. Sometimes, after meeting the target person but before going to sleep that night, some people found thoughts and ideas about the target person coming to mind, as well as feelings about what the target person's concern might be. Some people told me that, after hearing the group's dreams and the target person's concern the next day, they realized that their impressions from the day before often were correct. That was my clue that dreaming was not a requirement for intuition to work.

The Evaluation of Professional Psychics

"If wrong our hearts, our heads are right in vain."
                              Edward Young, *Night Thoughts*

My growing belief that compassion inspires a subjective intuition also received support from my experiences in another research project I conducted over those same years. As part of my consulting work with the A.R.E., I also have studied professional intuitives, who most of us call psychics. My colleague in this work was Carol Ann Liaros, author of the book, *Intuition Technologies*, and who is well qualified as a trainer, both by her experience as a professional intuitive and her involvement in laboratory ESP research.

Carol Ann and I were exploring the idea that it is possible to evaluate the performance of professional intuitives, not in an attempt to prove ESP, but in the more practical sense of evaluating their ability to help people solve problems. Could we tell the difference, we asked, between the "better" psychics and those who were less helpful?

As part of our work, Carol Ann and I each "auditioned" psychics who were applying to work at one of a series of A.R.E. conferences on intuition and psychic development. For the audition process, which usually took place via mail and recorded audiocassettes, Carol Ann and I each prepared a set of personal questions reflecting genuine dilemmas and ongoing problems in our respective lives.

We didn't ask "test" questions that served no helpful purpose beyond making the psychic "prove ESP." Instead, all our questions reflected a real need to know, which we felt would more authentically inspire the professional psychics' best efforts and also would more closely approximate what happens in the real world when people consult psychics. By submitting the same sets of questions to all the psychics, we could more easily compare their responses. That comparison proved very useful.

What we discovered was that we could make quite meaningful distinctions among the psychics. I noticed, for example, that some of the psychics provided me with more specific and useful information than did others. Some of the psychics were more inspiring than others. Some kept their responses limited to the questions while others went beyond the question itself to put their answers into a broader perspective. Still others seemed to bypass the question altogether. It was a pleasant surprise when Carol Ann and I compared our "ratings" of the psychics. We found we agreed, in the majority of the cases, on whom we considered to be the "best" psychics, those we gave ratings of "9" or "10." Thus, when it came to identifying the best psychics, two individuals could form a reliable agreement in their evaluations. That discovery in itself was a valuable breakthrough in that work, and we have continued to use the audition process to evaluate professional psychics who apply to work at the A.R.E. conferences.

Just as important, however, was another dimension to this research that also lingered in my mind. There was something about the psychic "auditions" that echoed what I had been seeing in the Dream Helper Ceremony. I noticed that the different psychics answered the same question with very different approaches. Concerning a question about my relationship with my father, for example, one psychic responded in terms of things I had done that made my relationship with my father more difficult. Another talked about past lives. Another used Biblical quotes. A fourth referred to passages from *A*

Check this out

Course in Miracles. Yet, each of the answers clearly related to my question, and each contained some helpful insight.

I realized that, even though these people were labeled "psychics," they were not peering into me with the objectivity of looking into a microscope. Instead, they were rendering creative impressions that reflected as much about the psychics themselves as they did about me. The overt content of their responses involved me and my life. But the choice of information, its organization, and its references all were expressions of the individual psychic's personal viewpoint. Yet, those whose responses I considered accurate touched me in ways that helped me see and understand things about myself, that had specific suggestions I could try, and that made me feel cared about and inspired.

In other words, when a group of psychics investigates an elephant, to borrow from a well-known allegorical story, they each psychically see "truth" that is dependent upon where on the "elephant" the psychic makes a connection and upon the psychic's own experiences. One sees the trunk, one the tail, one the ear, and so forth.

To understand the significance of this research for my discovery of the Intuitive Heart, it's important to look at two facts simultaneously. On the one hand, both Carol Ann and I, based upon independent evaluation, had selected a subgroup of the psychics as being "the best" and truly helpful. So they clearly had something positive to offer to the two of us experienced "clients." On the other hand, these psychic readings were not objective so much as they were personal statements by the psychics. Understanding this affirmed for me that it is possible to go within yourself and come up with something that, while it is a subjective impression, almost a personal confession of your point of view, nevertheless can touch the other person. In other words, you can produce insights with something like objective validity through this subjective process, and this process has merit.

A New Image for an Intuitive Counselor

"And I gave my heart to know wisdom, and to know madness and folly."   Ecclesiastes 1:17

At the same time that I found the consultations by the "best" psychics to be helpful, however, I also found them to be frustrating. It was clear to me that what I was getting was the psychics' efforts at translating their subjective impressions into more objective advice, probably because that's what most of their clients expect. Yet, I still could see enough of the subjective dimensions behind their statements that I felt almost cheated somehow at not being told the essential, ultimate truth, as the psychic knew it, but more of a packaged truth. I felt that I would receive "cleaner" information and guidance if the psychics did not try to translate their subjective impressions into more apparently objective terms, if they would, instead, confide in me, sincerely and directly, exactly what they experienced and were reminded of as they contemplated me and my questions.

My training as a counseling psychologist clicked in at this point. I asked myself, "If I were a counselor who also was a high-functioning psychic, how would I incorporate this ability into my counseling work?" I knew that I would not want to say to the client, "Here's what's wrong with you, here's your problem, here's where it came from, and here's what you need to do to fix it."

On the surface, it may seem like a fine thing to say to someone in order to solve their problem. It gets right to the point. It saves a lot of time spent digging in the client's psyche, into the past, wading through feelings, and so on. A lot of clients also would prefer such a straightforward approach. I know from personal experience, as well as from conversations with colleagues, that clients often ask for just such straightforward information. I can't count the number of times a client has said, "Okay, tell me straight, Doc. What's the matter with me?" But answering that question just as directly often is not as productive as it might appear to be.

Although one might think it would be a helpful and efficient approach to counseling to just tell people straight out what their problems are and what they should do for resolution, it really doesn't work that well. For one thing, people often don't take the advice they are given. If straightforward advice were the answer, the client probably already would have taken it, since they often already have heard the same advice from others. Instead, clients usually don't make the change until they experience for themselves the way out of their situation. People *need* to discover and experience their insights for themselves. They need to feel these truths as experienced realities, not as handed-down pronouncements. Experienced counselors appreciate this basic counseling truth, and it is why good counseling practice usually focuses primarily on helping clients make discoveries for themselves and use these discoveries to make their own changes. Rather than handing them fish, counselors prefer to teach "hungry" clients how to fish for themselves.

I continued to explore within myself for some intuitive guidance on how I would want to function as a "psychic counselor." When I incorporated my reflections on what I saw happening in the Dream Helper Ceremony, especially the kind of healing atmosphere that resulted from the group members sharing the personal side of their dreams for the target person, I began to get a sense of how, ideally, I could use intuitive ability to help some-one else.

A vision came to me of my ideal as an intuitive coun-selor. I saw my intuition working indirectly. What I imag-ined was that my intuitive connection with the client would cause personal stories about myself to come to me, stories that I would share with the client. The stories would reveal something about what I had learned from my own experience, but intuition would be at work in the selection and telling of the stories so that they also would help trigger my clients' awareness of their own growth possibilities.

What a simple answer! As a psychic, or intuitive coun-selor, I would *tell stories.* They would be personal but in-tuitively conceived stories that would hit the mark for the client. While being a storyteller didn't seem as pow-erful or as attractive as the image of the all-knowing psy-chic who could tell people everything they wanted to know, I already knew that, as attractive as that image might be, it was false. In theory, it sounded acceptable to let intuition function as a storyteller, but I wondered. Was it also a simplistic answer? Would it really work to help people?

Soon, I received important validation for the idea. It came, interestingly enough, from one of the professional psychics who had signed up for an audition. When she came for her appointment, she told me that, in fact, she really hadn't come for an audition. Instead, she said, she had come more out of curiosity about what we were do-ing. She said she no longer did psychic readings because she didn't like watching people grow dependent on her for answers. They didn't seem to be able to learn from her how to get their own answers. She wanted to know how Carol Ann and I handled that problem, since Edgar Cayce himself had been concerned that people should learn to search within themselves for their own answers.

But, she continued, once she got out of the "psychic" business, she began to notice something interesting happening, which she shared with me.

"I'll be having a conversation with someone," she explained, "and I'll tell them about something that once happened to me, and the person I'm talking to will say, 'Funny you should say that!' It will turn out that what I told them was just the story they needed to hear to help them with some concern or problem they had, even though they hadn't mentioned their problem at all."

"Well," I told her, laughing at the irony, "funny you should say that! You've just demonstrated what you've been talking about, because here you are validating for me an idea I've been having, and you've given me another idea about how to turn it into a concrete, formal training process."

As I spoke to her, still another idea came to me. I took a piece of paper, wrote down a question, folded it up and handed it to her.

"Let's see," I proposed, "whether you can do on purpose what you've been doing spontaneously. See if you can come up with a personal memory, a story that will relate to what I've written down here, in a helpful way."

She agreed to my game and took my folded paper. She held my question, unopened, for a moment and then began to speak. She told me that she now works as a travel agent and that she recently had been working on a proposal for a corporate client. She had worked very hard on it and wanted to do a good job, but the proposal grew and grew, and she had gotten very bogged down in it. She realized that she was getting into so much detail because she felt insecure about her ability to do the proposal and, as a result, she was trying to make it too perfect. She realized that she should just go back and do the basics, and when she did that, the proposal worked out fine.

Her story hit me hard. I had written on the piece of paper, "My book proposal." I had been worrying about whether I ever would get anything done with the proposal I had been working on for a book. I had gone through exactly the same experience with the proposal as she had. I had even used the same words as she. I had gotten into too much detail, had gotten bogged down, and was ready to abandon the project. Her story led me to examine whether some insecurity of my own was the cause of my problem and whether I needed to refocus the book idea, to get it down to its essence.

I gave the woman a big hug and thanked her profusely. I explained that she had helped me through the final stages of giving birth to a totally new way of training intuition, based upon what I knew was people's natural intuitive ability. When she left my office, I was very excited about what I now understood so clearly.

The *Ah Ha!* of the Intuitive Heart

"Hear with the understanding of the heart."
Thomas Vaughan, *Anima Magica Abscondita*

I immediately went outside for a meditative walk to pull my thoughts together. In the Dream Helper Ceremony, the dreams the dreamers offer come from inside themselves, are of and about themselves, and yet are related in surprising ways to the person they are trying to help. This was an important discovery, because it told me that, in reaching out to help another, we apparently are able to access a connection that isn't available when we stand apart from others and attempt to make judgmental statements about them or to diagnose their situation dispassionately.

There's a saying from the Talmud: "We don't see things as they are but as we are." We know ourselves, how we are, quite naturally and intuitively. Knowing ourselves, how we approach life and move through it, is an intuitive process of practical insight. When we care to help another, we can offer these insights honestly as self-insights and then be amazed at how they prove, paradoxically, to have objective, external value for the other person. A personal story, even a personal confession—which is what a dream is—proves to have value to another when the sincere intention is to be helpful. To elicit our natural intuitive ability, I realized, all we have to do is to reach out to another person in caring, and we will discover that we know more than we know we know. We can discover our intuitive ability.

What could I call this process of discovery, this vision of intuition? I wanted a clear image and name that would express not only its spirit, but also its meaning and its method. By the time I came back from the walk, I found that the phrase, "The Intuitive Heart" had come to me. I smiled a great "Ah Ha!"

You can have this same kind of discovery experience. What excites me so much about my discovery is that it can help you recognize and appreciate something you already have.

What I'm sharing with you is an intuitive approach to your own intuition.

The technique I'm going to use in this book to teach you how to connect with your own Intuitive Heart will help you learn to appreciate and trust more in your own natural intuitive abilities. You'll grow into greater comfort with them so that they become a workable, serviceable tool in your life.

The training technique is very simple: *Start by helping others.*

There are several important reasons to approach learning about your Intuitive Heart this way. Helping others helps you learn to get out of your own way, which can be a real stumbling block to intuition. Another person's concern can motivate you in a way that your own concerns can't. Helping another person also gives you an objective outsider whose response to your efforts can provide you with external validation that your intuition is trustworthy.

As this training process begins to make more sense to you, to feel more natural, as your intuition begins to speak to you, you then will be able to use it to help yourself. I'll show you how to do that as well.

My whole thesis in this book, the whole theme of the Intuitive Heart, is that you already carry within you a natural intuitive ability. It comes out in subtle ways, but I have developed a method you can use to explore this ability, to see it, and to examine it. And to see that it *works.*

In chapter three, I will briefly explain the Intuitive Heart discovery process to give you an overview of how to do it. In subsequent chapters, I'll also give you more detailed information about each of the steps in this method and opportunities to practice each step. This information will become more meaningful once you actually are practicing with your intuitive ability. Finally, I'll show you how to take what you've learned and use it to help yourself. You will find your own Intuitive Heart to be a trustworthy guide.

3

The Intuitive Heart
Discovery Process

The heart has its reasons which reason knows nothing of. We know the truth, not only by reason, but by the heart.

Blaise Pascal, *Pensees No. 4*

After learning to use the Intuitive Heart discovery process that follows, Pepe was anxious to try out his newly found ability. He asked his friend, Demetri, to help him.

Pepe explained that he was experimenting with his intuitive storytelling skills. He would, he said, intuitively draw upon his personal memories and make a story out of one of them. He would make it a teaching story, something to learn from, by adding his own reflections on what lessons the memory taught him. Pepe said he hoped the story might touch Demetri in some way, maybe even be pertinent to one of Demetri's personal concerns. Demetri agreed to think of some question or challenge he faced, something that he cared about, without telling Pepe what it was.

Pepe held Demetri in his heart for a moment of silence. He then explained that a memory came to him of his childhood in Yugoslavia. Pepe's father worked in East Germany and came home about once a year. Without his father around, Pepe was used to playing alone. He remembered a particular day when he was playing with his toys and his father arrived on an unexpected visit.

"I ran up and gave him a big hug," Pepe said. "I told him, 'Papa, come and see what I've made with my toys!' My father said he was impressed, and then he played with me. I was so proud that, while he was away, I had created something that he approved of." As Pepe reflected on the memory and the wisdom it might teach, he said it reminded him of the importance of taking initiative on his own and using his own abilities to their fullest, and that good surprises and rewards can come later as a result of his efforts.

Demetri became very excited at Pepe's story. He revealed that he secretly had thought of this question: "Should I start up my new business selling greeting cards?"

"I pray to God about this new business," Demetri explained. "But God doesn't answer. I don't win the lottery. I don't find money. And I've been almost angry that my prayers are ignored. But in your story, you started something on your own, and then your father came and blessed it. I realize that I must start myself to get this business going, and then perhaps God will bless my efforts."

Pepe, who said he had almost pushed the memory away because it hadn't seemed like much, was pleased to hear how it touched Demetri.

When they met again a couple of months later, Demetri had started his own business, and it was going well. He thanked Pepe for telling him just the story he needed to hear.

What Pepe was able to do for his friend, you can do, too. Using the Intuitive Heart discovery process, you can find, from your own memories and experiences, stories that inspire important truths, insights, and wisdom. You will be able to discover within yourself a source of guidance that makes a difference in your own life and in the lives of those around you. You'll discover that your own Intuitive Heart has a special wisdom that seems almost magical, yet is perfectly natural.

First, the training will begin by taking you through the Intuitive Heart discovery process step by step. You'll start by practicing some enjoyable steps in relaxation and feeling good. These are very natural procedures, once you understand them, and very important for placing you in the most conducive frame of mind to promote your natural intuition.

You then will continue your training with the help of a cooperating partner. You can enlist the aid of anyone who has a question or concern with which you want to help. It's simple and easy to do, and as you practice it, you will see that it works. It's easier to begin learning the intuition process by working with a partner, let me assure you, than it is to begin working with yourself alone. For one thing, your natural intuition is activated most easily by a desire to help someone else. Later, I'll explain

*me + Paula

some additional reasons why working with a partner is so helpful. I'll also describe all the special power that lies behind each of the steps. Understanding what goes on "behind the scenes" can make your practice more meaningful and even more effective.

The six steps of the Intuitive Heart discovery process are briefly introduced below. You don't have to worry at this point about actually doing the steps. Just read the brief summaries of each one to get an overall picture of what the process involves. Once you have the big picture, we will revisit the steps in much greater detail by devoting an entire chapter to each one and letting you practice as we go along. You soon will discover that each step contains a wealth of surprises and benefits for you.

- **Step One: Learn from Your Breath—You Can Trust in Inspiration**

"Let the counsel of thine own heart stand."   Matthew 37:13

Focus on your breathing and discover how you can trust it to flow naturally, spontaneously, with no effort or control on your part. Intuitive inspiration will come to you the same way.

When you have chosen a partner and the two of you are comfortably seated facing each other, have your partner think about the question or concern, even writing it down if that helps your partner hold it in awareness.

You are ready to begin, by learning to shift "gears" and move into a frame of mind that is receptive to intuition. To begin making this shift, gently focus your attention on your breathing.

Attention to your breathing can help to move your

awareness into a type of "flow" state—as in the "flow" of your breathing. This shift in consciousness is an important first step. Although your intention is to be helpful through your intuitive ability, we already know that working at being intuitive can get in the way. Intuition is at its best when it comes naturally. Probably the most natural, effortless, flowing thing going on within each of us is our breathing. By moving your awareness to your breath, you can shift that awareness into a more natural, receptive, effortless state.

Try it for a moment. Focus on your breathing. Gently pay attention to it. Be mindful of it. If it helps to close your eyes, do so.

On the exhalations, allow yourself to relax. On the inhalations, accept the breath coming to you naturally, without your making any effort yourself.

Think to yourself, "I can trust the inspiration." Remember that inspiration means both the natural entering of the breath and the new, creative idea. As you relax into your breath, be aware that you are relaxing into some higher process. Be thankful for this wonderful gift, the gift of breath and life.

Enjoy this state of "flow" for as long as you like.

• Step Two: Make The Heart Connection

"The heart has such an influence over the understanding that it is worthwhile to engage it in our interest." Lord Chesterfield, *Letters*

Let gratitude fill your heart, allowing you to release all concerns. Your heart energy naturally begins to expand. Focus it on the target of your search for intuition. Make a heart connection with whatever it is about which you wish to be intuitive. Hold it with compassion and empathy.

As you begin to enjoy the feeling of being grateful for the gift of your breath, you will notice that a mood shift has been taking place. The more you enjoy this experience, the more your mood becomes positive, mellow, serene, easy-going, and receptive.

As feelings of gratitude become more perceptible and your mood shift becomes more evident, move your awareness to the area of your heart. In a few moments, you may feel as if your heart is softening, becoming warm, or expanding. Imagine that what you are feeling is love blossoming in your heart. This love may feel very real.

As the feeling of love grows within your awareness, imagine that this feeling reaches out very naturally to include the presence of the person or concern about whom or which you wish to be intuitive. Imagine that your feeling of love has surrounded the other person, or that you can feel or hear or see your question being surrounded by the love in your heart. (For much of the training, this other presence will be the person whose concern you wish to address, to whom you wish to tell a helpful story. Later it will be yourself, your own concerns or interests, that will be the focus of your Intuitive Heart.) Allow yourself to experience a heart connection between the two of you.

The experience of the flowering or radiating heart, as well as the experience of a heart connection with another person, arise much more naturally than it might seem simply from reading the words on the page without doing the actual practice. As you actually do the practice, I assure you that the written guidance I will provide will combine with your own experience to introduce you to a reality that is quite vivid and reliable. Keep my promise in mind as I continue outlining the steps of the process.

For a moment, simply enjoy the heart connection with the other person. Love flows through you, and you share that love with the other person. Let this love push aside all concerns, making worry seem pointless. Simply experience the feeling of love. Trust in inspiration. Realize that while you have a purpose to fulfill, a mission to accomplish on behalf of the other person, that you can, nevertheless, relax. You can trust that the same inspiration you are enjoying in your breath will naturally bring to you everything you need. Discover what a good feeling it is to accept such confidence. You'll soon find out that you are not simply making flowery affirmations, but are being guided onto a path of profound discovery.

- **Step Three: Invite a Memory**

"Great thoughts always come from the heart."

Marquis de Vauvenargues,
Reflexions et maximes

Ask for one of your millions of personal memories to pop into your mind. Without intentionally choosing it, but accepting the first one that comes, trust that within your heart is stored the perfect memory that is just right for this occasion.

You will discover that you can trust that, without any effort on your part, just the right memory from among your many life experiences will come to you. Intuitively, the most helpful of your experiences will be drawn into the heart connection between you and your partner. In your state of gratitude and trust, no effort is necessary. You don't need to try to anticipate what memory will come or should come. You can be indifferent to what the

memory might be like, whether it is seemingly important or apparently trivial, depressing or happy. It doesn't
matter. You don't need to evaluate the memory that does
come.

Each of your breaths is different, yet perfect for the
moment. It feels good to accept each one as it comes.
You can do the same with the flow of your mind, trusting
and accepting the memory that comes.

If you like, you can think along the lines of this affirmation to focus the quality of your awareness at this moment:

> *I trust in inspiration. Guided by love and trusting
> inspiration, I now allow a memory to come to me, a
> recollection of a specific experience from my past.
> When I tell this memory aloud as a story and reflect
> upon the meaning it has for me today, my sharing
> will inspire in my partner exactly the necessary wis-
> dom required for whatever concern my partner's
> heart is holding.*

How can you go wrong with an attitude like that? In
this attitude of naturalness and loving helpfulness, just
allow a memory to come. Don't search or struggle for
one. Don't push away whatever comes to you. Don't pass
judgment on its quality. Just accept whatever memory
appears to you.

• Step Four: Tell Your Story

"Out of the abundance of the heart the mouth speaketh."
                                        Matthew 12:34

*Explore the experience that surrounds that memory.
Let your memory be the seed of a story—here's what*

was going on, here's what happened, here's how it turned out.

Having accepted the first memory that popped into your mind, open your eyes, if you have had them closed, and begin to speak to your partner. Using this memory as your starting point, tell your partner the story of what happened. Describe the scene, and as you describe it, talk about what was going on for you at the time of that memory. Just enjoy your telling of this story: the setting, some tension, what happened, and then how things worked out in some particular way.

What could be easier than telling the story of what happened to you? Everyone loves to tell stories. It's very easy and natural. We all do it all the time.

Telling and listening to stories is not only easy and natural, but as we'll see, intuition also is very much alive when we do so. Telling a story is good fun. Enjoy it. The more you enjoy it, the more intuition will be present.

• Step Five: Search Your Heart for Wisdom

"I communed with mine own heart, saying, Lo, I am come to great estate, and have gotten more wisdom than all [they] that have been before me in Jerusalem: yea, my heart had great experience of wisdom and knowledge."   Ecclesiastes 1:16

See what lessons your story holds. What truths does it contain? What did you learn from that experience? What does this story teach you today?

When you've told the story, ask yourself aloud so your partner can hear, "What can I learn from this story for myself? What does it have to teach me at this moment?" Do your thinking aloud so your partner can listen. Explore the meaning the story has for you by talking it out.

In a caring way, search your heart for wisdom about this memory. Look back on your past and how you've grown since then. As you share your thoughts, it's very natural and very much okay not to know where you're headed with the whole thing. It's okay and very intuitive to be talking and yet not to know what the particular point of it all might be. Just say what is in your heart and mind in an extemporaneous way, sincerely, spontaneously, keeping your awareness in the flow state and with the attitude of, "I am searching my heart for wisdom to understand what I can learn from this, listening to what my heart tells me in hopes that my sincere offering will be useful to my partner."

Because you care, you are willing to share the wisdom that you discover from your story. And even you may be surprised at some of the things you find in the story that you did not suspect were there when you started.

• Step Six: Learn from Feedback

"Heart speaks to heart."   Cardinal Newman

Note how the teaching story relates to the focus of your quest for intuition. How can you use this new perspective to respond to your current situation differently?

When you have finished with your story and the lessons it held for you, ask your partner for some feedback. You may ask whether your partner was touched by any part of your story and whether your partner would be willing to tell you about that. Usually, that's all you need to say, and most people will really open up at this point. Most will tell you what their question or concern was. If they don't (sometimes they are so excited by your story that they forget), you may ask if they would mind sharing the question with you.

My experience is that usually people will share both their question and the impact of your story because you have been so open and willing to share so much of yourself. And what I fully expect you will hear is how pertinent your memory and the story you told about it are to the question or concern your partner had.

You probably will find yourself in an intimate conversation with your partner. You'll both be as surprised as Pepe and Dimitri to discover how important your simple story really is. You'll find you have some interesting things in common with each other, things you might not have suspected but which intuition brought to the surface. You'll find out just how much you have to learn from each other. And you'll discover that you can trust your intuition. That's the discovery we want you to remember and to repeat as often as necessary until you can really accept it. Your partners are going to be very helpful in that discovery process.

A Simple Method Has Profound Results

"If you want to know yourself,
Just look how others do it;
If you want to understand others,
Look into your own heart."
> Johann Christoph Friedrich von Schiller, *Tabulae Votivae*

Well, that's it. That's the Intuitive Heart discovery process. There is nothing complicated, difficult, or mysterious about it. In fact, the only problem you may have is some initial awkwardness about learning to relax into your breathing, about feeling so good in your heart, or about involving a partner to practice your intuitive storytelling technique. But the more times you go through the Intuitive Heart discovery process, the more natural it will become for you, and you will begin to make several discoveries.

You will discover that the breath can introduce you to more than just the flow state. You'll discover that experiencing a heart connection with other people has some secrets to reveal. You'll discover that your memories are richer than you would believe and seem to have an intelligence of their own, and you'll wonder how they know which one should come to you.

All these discoveries will form a body of personalized information that will be a teacher for you. They will guide you in developing your Intuitive Heart skills. There is so much to learn from each of these steps, in addition to the intuitive skill you will be developing, that we will talk in detail about all these things in the following chapters.

Before going on to those chapters, however, I have one last word about inviting partners to help you practice. You may discover that you have a certain amount of shyness in approaching even close friends or family to do this work. And that's perfectly okay. Let the shyness be there, if it is, because inside each of us is a part that is reluctant, that has fears about exposure, about being wrong, about looking foolish. In fact, they are all those same fears that people mention when they talk about regretting not following a hunch. So bring your doubts with you to this process, because they need to be touched by the enthusiasm, the joy, the pleasure, and the insights that can come from it.

This is something that you will need to see for yourself, experience in your own heart and physical body and in your connections with others, in order for it to come

alive and be real for you. As we go, I will tell you about
my own experiences as well as those of others, but again,
you will need to experience it for yourself.

Also, as we look at the Intuitive Heart discovery process in a little more detail, you'll notice that I'm teaching
you the steps.

4

Step One:
Learn from Your Breath—
You Can Trust Inspiration

"For mercy has a human heart."

William Blake, *Songs of Innocence*

*I*n the midst of her anger, Michelle noticed she was squeezing down on her breathing. Then she remembered a simple breathing technique for redirecting the energy. Her chest was constricted. She drew a deep breath and, slowly and carefully, she took in some complete, fulfilling breaths. Then she sighed in relief.

Eventually, Michelle forgot to think about how deeply she was breathing. She just let it happen on its own. She found herself watching it happen, felt her lungs draw in air, and felt a movement of energy throughout her body. Then, the old air left her lungs, taking her tension and fatigue with it. As she continued to watch, she noticed that, just for a moment between one breath leaving and another coming in, everything paused. Then, miraculously, the next breath came, right on time, in its own time, of its own accord.

"I have never felt so in touch with my body," Michelle said. "It was tranquil and exhilarating at the same time, a very special moment for me, almost a peak experience."

Several thoughts went through Michelle's mind. She thought about the fight she had had with her husband that morning. She realized she had gotten mad because he hadn't done something for her that she had assumed he would.

"I realized just how much I had come to take him for granted," Michelle explained. "I could feel just how unappreciated he was feeling."

What would happen, Michelle wondered, if she gave to her husband a little appreciation when he did something for her, even when it was something she expected him to do, like the appreciation she was feeling for her breath, something she also had taken for granted? It would prove to be a transforming thought for her and for her marriage.

The Secret of Flow

"Give all to love;
Obey thy heart;
Friends, kindred, days,
Estate, good fame,
Plans, credit and the Muse,
Nothing refuse."
          Ralph Waldo Emerson
          Ode Inscribed to W.H. Channing, *Give All to Love,* st.1

In her moment of inspiration, Michelle stumbled onto a secret of intuition. Maybe sometimes you have taken a "breather" and gained a fresh new perspective. Taking time out is an important step in dealing intuitively with a situation. But there's something else that Michelle stumbled upon that's just as important. In falling into the flow of her breathing, she also naturally tapped into an intelligence larger than her own.

If you've ever watched champion tennis, basketball, or soccer players in action, you've probably noticed how quickly they respond to events. What's more, every move evolves rapidly, one move flowing into the next. They are champions of instant improvisation. Even with all their planning and practice, there is little they can do by rote; it's all made up on the spot. When they are at their best, these athletes play in a state of constant inspiration. There is usually little time to think consciously about what to do next; they just respond intuitively. When they experience peak moments of especially graceful play, when it seems to happen effortlessly, they say they are in "the zone," where nothing goes wrong, or in the "flow," where the play happens by itself.

You may remember experiencing some moments of flow in your own life. Maybe everything just fell into place. Errands worked themselves out as if choreographed by the city planner. You found yourself in the right place at the right time as if everyone knew your schedule. Obstacles melted away as if life were handing you the keys to the kingdom.

The term "flow" entered the academic and popular vocabulary as the result of research by Mihaly Csikszentmihalyi, a University of Chicago psychology professor, who has spent years studying this state of mind. According to Csikszentmihalyi, we all experience states of flow in many aspects of our lives—athletics, creative endeavors, relationships, our connectedness with the world around us. When we are doing what comes naturally, we are usually doing it gracefully. Even simple acts, simple moments, can have their natural grace as they ride along the flow of the experience.

Csikszentmihalyi describes flow as a state of "optimal experience." It is where you are completely focused, your concentration bringing you total absorption in the activity that has your attention. It is a state of consciousness that focuses your energy and attention and seems to carry you along as if moved by an outside force.

If you have ever been so absorbed in an activity—music, reading, painting, or a project at your job, perhaps—that you were carried along by the spirit of that activity, losing all track of time and anything else going on around you, then you were in flow. If you have ever found yourself, during a walk, suddenly shifting into a more intense connection with the physical world around you, then you were in flow.

On the other hand, when we are outside the flow, life can be quite effort-filled. It is almost as if we look about us, not quite sure what to do, what we want, what is expected of us. It is like a sail boat caught in the "doldrums," where there is no wind to fill the sails, and so the boat sits there, helplessly dead in the water. If there is any pressure to perform, then even worse than the doldrums is the ensuing sense of stage fright, the anxiety of being caught short and lacking. Here self-consciousness is a state of extreme painfulness.

The flow state is the opposite of the doldrums. Self-consciousness becomes the joy of watching your experience unfold before you. Everything moves along effortlessly; everything comes out right seemingly automatically.

According to Csikszentmihalyi's research, flow seems to result from several things: focused attention, the ability to do something well, training and practice, letting yourself go into what you are doing, becoming one with it. In a state of flow, you feel more like yourself, your natural self, more like you are doing what you are meant to be doing.

Whatever the circumstances of your own experience with flow, you probably will agree that it was as if you somehow relaxed into the experience and let it take on a life of its own, as if you got out of your own way. At the time, if you had stopped to think about it, it probably all would have seemed very natural.

Flow is a natural state and, thus, it is no surprise that it has received recognition in older traditions than scientific psychology. One of the earliest champions of the reality of flow was Taoism, a very ancient philosophy from China. Taoism is founded on the "Tao," meaning "The Way," which is the path of flow. Another way of describing the Tao is to say, "the way things are." When you are in harmony with the way things are, then things just work out for you, naturally, effortlessly. In harmony with the Tao, you are connected to the larger intelligence of the universe. When you are in harmony with the Tao, in the flow, your natural intuition is amplified beyond your own understanding. Here you can, to paraphrase a popular song, know things without knowing why.

Csikszentmihalyi's research confirms that during those moments of flow, people evidence greater intuition. You probably often have seen for yourself that it is easier to be intuitive in the little things during your day, especially when you aren't trying to be. But as soon as you make an effort to be intuitive or feel that something important is at stake, you find yourself blocked, full of self-doubt. When I ask people, almost everyone agrees that it is easier to be intuitive when they're not thinking about it. In fact, when we stop to think about it, we can't be intuitive—or so it seems.

There is a way past this block. Learning how to get past this negative feeling of self-consciousness will be very important, and enjoyable, too! You can learn to enter the flow intentionally, and it's your breath that's going to show you the way.

The Breath Has a Natural Flow

"And the heart must pause to breath . . . "
Lord Byron, *So We'll Go No More A-Roving*

I've learned that the breath really can be a fine teacher in your study of intuition. It has many lessons to teach you, and it can be a meaningful guide into some important intuitive realms that are hard to reach otherwise.

For one thing, the breath can teach you how to enter the flow state deliberately and with full awareness. Through the breath, you can gain entrance to an intuitive mind space that usually is reserved for moments when you aren't thinking about it.

To begin learning the breath's secrets about flow and intuition, the first thing to do is to explore what it's like to pay attention to your breath while also letting it happen naturally. You can do this even as you're reading these pages. There's no need to stop reading, although it's fine to stop at any point, if you wish, in order to become even more absorbed in watching your breath. Just be aware of your breathing, allowing it to happen naturally, spontaneously, doing whatever it will do, without your trying to affect it.

If you're like most people, you'll find that, as soon as you begin to pay attention to the breath, you begin to affect it, worry about it, change it, make it different, evaluate it. When I introduce people to observing their breath while letting it be, they usually find they feel a need to change their breathing in some way. Once they begin to focus on their breath, they experience almost a compulsive need to control it.

People sometimes tell me that when they focus on the breath, they suddenly feel that their breathing is too shallow and they want to breathe more deeply. Others say they feel fear that the breath won't happen if they don't make it happen with their own effort, as if their usual ability to breath automatically freezes up. People who have had yoga training often say that they find themselves guiding their breathing to a slow, rhythmic count. Whatever their experience, most people initially find themselves imposing some influence on their breathing, stepping into the middle of it to affect it in some way.

This tendency to interfere with the natural flow of the breath is certainly a curiosity. Think about it. You have been breathing for years without having to make it happen, just letting it happen by itself without paying much attention to it. And yet, as soon as you focus your attention on the breath, you seem to feel a need to control it or fix it or influence it in some way. Even though we all know that it really isn't necessary, that the breath will happen by itself, we can't help but try to control it.

This dilemma is the same predicament that we've seen happen with intuition. When you go with the "flow" of your daily life, acting improvisationally and doing what "feels" like the right thing to do, acting spontaneously without thinking about it, you are being intuitive, and it's easy and natural. It's only when you start to focus on intuition, when you try to make it happen on call, that you begin to analyze it, try to control it, worry that it won't happen on it's own. And then you get in intuition's way.

Yet, you will discover, the irony is that the secret to intuition is very simple. The secret is hidden in your breathing. But once you discover it, you will realize that it's been there all along, in plain sight. It's hidden now because, even though you may look at it, you may not see it. *The secret to intuition is: Let yourself be. Just let yourself be yourself. Just act naturally.*

This secret may not sound like much of a revelation, but as we go through the Intuitive Heart discovery process, you will come to appreciate, as I have, what many people have told me. As they come to accept and reclaim their own natural intuitive style or ability, it's as if they come to accept and claim themselves at a newer and deeper level. A well-respected professional intuitive, Caroline Myss, once remarked, "The only block to your natural intuition is low self-esteem." My students have found that this statement has proven true for them. It is an important idea that you would do well to keep in mind until the day you realize its truth: Being intuitive is being yourself in a very profound way. Now, let's go back to the breath.

Keep in mind that you've been breathing without effort all your life. It happens naturally. Now you can learn to let it continue to be natural even when you are paying attention to it. Nothing more, nothing less. The goal simply is to be yourself, mindful of yourself. What you're going to do is use the process of learning to trust in the flow of the breath to see what it brings you. It can bring you to your goal.

Your Breath Can Teach You to Relax

"A merry heart goes all the day"
                    William Shakespeare, *The Winter's Tale.*

The breath is a teacher. Watch your breathing as you let it be. Simply follow it without worrying about it or changing it. Notice that on the exhalations, when your breath goes out, there is a very natural relaxation. Let your breath show you how it relaxes. Let it teach you about letting go. Watch how the muscles in the chest and stomach area let go and relax on the exhalation. Let your exhalations help you to let go.

After doing this for a while, this feeling of relaxation may call something up for you. When I ask people what this feeling is like for them, they often use words such as softening, a balloon that's deflating, the wind going out of sails, or loosening. Think about what feelings and images come for you during the letting go of the exhalations.

What is letting go? What actually happens in the exhalation? If you look at it closely, you will see that what the lungs do is exactly nothing. That is, they collapse, and the air leaves. Letting go is releasing.

You can explore this same idea for yourself with your fist. Squeeze your hand into a tight fist. Now, just let it go. What did you do to accomplish this letting go? You stopped doing anything, right? (Where does your fist go, by the way, when you relax your hand? This is a good question to ask kids just to see the looks on their faces as they try to figure out the puzzle.) Squeeze your hand into a fist again. Let it go. Tense, release. This sequence of first squeezing and then letting go of muscles throughout the body is a basic relaxation training technique. The same thing happens with the breath.

By paying attention to your exhalations, you can let your breath teach you how to relax, to release, to let go. And if you stumble over it at first, don't worry. You'll soon get past any awkwardness, and then your breath can be your guide to other learning about being in the flow and about accepting natural intuition.

As you become more comfortable letting yourself go as the breath exhales, you'll probably notice further qualities of the experience.

When I ask people to tell me what comes to mind as they relax more deeply with the breath, they typically mention images such as drifting, falling asleep, dissolving, waves disappearing in the sand upon the beach, evaporating, or disappearing in peace.

Some people have reported that letting go fully with the exhalations feels like a little death. They have a sort of "near-death" experience while they watch it happen. They find it very exciting to experiment with letting go that much. It reminds them of times as a child when, on the playground swing, they experimented with taking risks and letting themselves go into the thrill of the swing.

The breath can be a profound relaxer, helping you to find your own way to get out of your way and become one with the flow.

Your Breath Can Teach You to Trust

> "Your vision will become clear only when you look into your heart."
> Carl Jung

Exhaling isn't the only thing going on in your breathing. The breath also comes in on the inhalations. Shift your attention, focusing on these inhalations. Continue to allow your breathing to happen on its own. Let it be as you wait for the inhalations. Let them come on their own.

As you watch your exhalations, you probably will notice that you relax a little more with each breath that goes out. As that happens, you may notice as well that your increasing ability to let go also brings with it a certain trust, trust that another breath will come to replace what you just released.

Let the inhalations show you how to accept them as they come. Let the inhalations show you how to trust. Let that next breath come to you, trusting that it will come as it is needed, accepting that it comes of its own accord.

As you observe your inhalations, notice what comes to mind. People tell me that their inhalations feel like a balloon filling up, like being lifted up or awakened. Accepting fully the breath coming in on its own has its special pleasures. Some people describe it in sexual terms, as bringing special delight.

It is surprising that something so common and close to you can bring such joy. In combination with profound letting go, the experience of trusting that the next breath will come and of yielding to the breath when it does come, can create its own ecstasy. You can feel as if life itself is taking you into its flow. Such a deep encounter with trust can be very healing. It also will help you reach deeper levels of your intuitive gifts.

You Can Meditate on Your Breath's Wisdom

"The human heart has hidden treasures,
In secret kept, in silence sealed."
                    Charlotte Brontë, *Evening Solace*, st.1

It may seem silly to make such a big deal out of something as natural as the breath, but there are great rewards to come from experiencing profound gratitude for the simple things. It also affects the mood in a way that invites deep intuitive powers.

So just practice watching your breath. Relax more with each exhalation, letting it go. Trust that the next breath will come, accepting it as it does. As you become more comfortable and absorbed in the flow of your breathing, notice again what it feels like for you, what images or associations come to you.

People often tell me they think about being at the seashore, about the natural rhythm of the waves, with each wave following its own natural inclination. Others speak of a feeling of being rocked, comforted, held, of being given sustenance through the breath's gift of life. Some talk about feeling at one with the breath, of merging with and becoming a part of everything.

Following the breath into pleasurable states of consciousness can be fun. Seeing what mental pictures come to describe your experiences can be a great game. But it's more than just fun and games. You are making three very important discoveries.

First, with your exhalations, you are learning how your breath can help you relax. In fact, you are learning about just how profound letting go can be, and how you can enjoy experiencing it.

Second, with your inhalations, you are learning how your breath can teach you to accept something happening spontaneously within you. You are learning to tune into the state of natural flow. In fact, as you continue to explore this experience, you will discover how the secrets of intuition are hidden within that flow.

Third, by paying attention to the thoughts, feelings and images that come to mind, you are learning to tune into your intuition. That's what experiencing intuition is all about: paying attention to the flow of your inner experience. From within yourself arise visions of understanding about the mystery of breath. Soon you will find that from within yourself there will arise flashes of insight about other aspects of life.

As you practice being mindful of your breath (and it's something you can practice almost anywhere at any time), these types of images will become more familiar to you. And they are instructive not only about the breath, but also about intuition. In fact, these feelings of being at one with the universe, of merging with that which surrounds you, point you toward an explanation of why there can be such a thing as intuition in the first place. It has to do—and we will explore this further later—with the fact that you and the universe are connected in some way and that, inside yourself, you can tap into understanding, wisdom, and knowledge about the world outside yourself.

Don't be surprised if you don't have these experiences the very first time you try following your breath. But these experiences, or something similar, will come with practice. So let's give you a chance to practice some more and talk about what the experience is like. Go through the process again, and let's explore it more thoroughly. You'll soon see that each time, your breath has new things to teach you.

Your Breath Teaches You Secrets of Intuition

"It is my heart that makes my songs . . . "   Sara Teasdale

Continue to practice being mindful of your breath and watching what comes to mind. You will learn how to both tune in and let go at the same time. You learn that lesson by relaxing control so that you can give the breath your attention without the need to make it happen through any conscious effort.

Let the exhalations teach you how to relax and let go. Let the inhalations teach you to trust and accept. You are learning the secret of trust, trust in your breath and its inspiration. You are learning to trust and receive inspiration by tuning in, letting go, and accepting what comes.

This exploration is important practice in discovering your intuitive abilities. As you become more accustomed to the idea that you can focus within, that you can tune in and concentrate inside, while at the same time allowing things to unfold naturally and spontaneously, you also are teaching yourself to be intentionally intuitive.

Think about it: Tune in, let go, accept intuition. Perhaps you can see, or guess, that a formula is developing here.

When you wish to be intuitive, you need to turn inward to look for your intuitions because that's the place from which they come. At the same time, you need to allow the flow of consciousness to happen spontaneously and naturally. That's what you're doing in your practice with the breath. As you practice and learn, enjoying the breath, remind yourself how the breath can be a teacher, can guide you into relaxing and letting go, can teach you about trust and acceptance.

As you practice with the breath, notice the small pauses between the last of the air leaving your lungs and the next breath coming in. In that moment, you might wonder, where does the breath come from? When will it happen? Somewhere in that split second, the new breath is born. Isn't that wonderful? Isn't it a magical moment? Enjoy this gift of life that is creating and guiding your breathing. It's happening in everyone who breathes. It's right here, right now, for you.

This practice with the breath can be a lot of fun and very relaxing. It's interesting to focus on the breath, to think about it's mystery and magic, to ask these kinds of questions, and see what answers your breath brings. The breath has much in the way of wisdom to share with you.

Now, I'm going to describe for you two really interesting ideas to explore with the help of your breath's wisdom and its ability to facilitate your intuition.

The Mystery of Inspiration

"The best and most beautiful things in the world cannot be seen or even touched. They must be felt with the heart."   Helen Keller

Inspiration itself is a fun mystery to explore. Here's what I mean: As you practice following your breath in trust and relaxation, let that word, *inspiration,* float around in your mind. Let your breath think about what the word means. It's an interesting word because it means both the natural coming in of a breath and the creative arrival of new ideas.

As the breath comes in by itself, meditate on the dual meaning of inspiration.

Let your breath bring you an image of what it means to you. Why do we use the same word for breathing that we use for having creative ideas come to us? What does your intuition say? When I ask people to report what comes to mind, some say they see it as a light bulb turning on from the electricity that is flowing through it, and that they, likewise, light up from an inspiration. Inspiration, some say, is like being filled with ideas, like being filled with air: It's exciting, invigorating, and when it happens, it's a surprise, but it happens all the time. Other people tell me that an inspiration is something that comes into you from outside, an idea that seems to come to you from out of nowhere. One person imagined it was like the sunlight shining on a plant, on all the plants, causing them to flower, each in their own way. The common thread that runs through all the descriptions I hear is that, although inspirations happen within us, they come to us from beyond, on their own impulse, as if they are special gifts to us from afar, planted within us.

Inspiration seems to come from outside you, and yet it happens within you. Do you realize that, in both senses of the word, you are experiencing inspiration constantly? Inspiration is so natural that you may not have recognized it and appreciated it for the mystery and magic that it is. It's an idea you will meet again and again in your work with intuition. It's a fun mystery and also something of a paradox, a contradiction. It can fill you with wonder and make you scratch your head at the same time. How can something come from outside or beyond us, and yet happen within us? You can scratch your head about it, or maybe meditate on your breath, to come up with your own answer to this paradox. It's something that is so natural and yet so mysterious and magic, so full of potential for exploration. It's from beyond you, yet it happens within you. Just like intuition?

Discovering the Spirit in the Breath

"I feel my heart new open'd."

William Shakespeare, *King Henry the Eighth*

The second idea to explore in your meditation on the breath is spirit.

In my teaching, I ask people to continue following their breathing with relaxation and acceptance, and to let their breath suggest to them ideas about spirit. Simply ask your breath how it is like spirit, and let the breath deliver its inspirations. It doesn't matter if you don't think you know the answer; just see what your intuition says.

Although people puzzle over such deep questions, they are surprised that they find answers arising suddenly from within themselves, coming to them on their breath. Breath has brought many creative answers to this question. I've heard many fascinating, even poetic, "inspirations" about the connection between breath and spirit.

Spirit, some tell me, is a life force that animates us, much as the breath, as the air does. So, like the air, the wind, when the breath comes in, we are filled with spirit. Like the wind, this spirit is invisible, but it still has the power to bring life. And some remind me that we all share the same air, the same spirit, because we are filled with breath, a oneness that connects us to each other.

A few people report that they see a cloud in the sky in the shape of a face, like a god, blowing air into them.

People's inspirations, their own intuitions, seem to be connected to ideas from our deep history. The words themselves, both *inspiration* and *spirit,* come from the Latin word *spiritus*, which means breath, soul, life. In practically every religious and spiritual tradition, in fact, the breath is linked with spirit and with spirit's role as the source of all life.

The Polynesian model of health, for example, is expressed in the Hawaiian greeting, "Aloha!" This familiar word means "sharing the sacred breath given us by the Creator," according to Paul Ka'ikena Pearsall, Ph.D., author of *A Healing Intimacy: The Power of Loving Connections.*

You, too, can follow the paths by which the soul of humanity has placed on the breath an echo of the spirit. As you continue to follow your breath, see what images and thoughts come to you. You may make some interesting discoveries of your own about spirit in the breath, and these discoveries will help you to connect more fully with the spiritual dimension of intuition and the development of your Intuitive Heart.

Practice Inspirational Breathing to Improve Intuition

"Give your ears to hear the sayings,
Give your heart to understand them . . . "

Amenemope

Teaching people this technique of following the breath is one of my favorite things because, even before we've gotten to working directly with intuition, we already have been given some special gifts: The good feelings of relaxation and learning to trust, and the ideas and connections that come to us as we watch the breath. As you practice more and more, you, too, will find that your breath has much to say to you about that trust and those new ideas, and about new ways of experiencing your life, of being in the world.

Best of all, these gifts can be yours almost any time. You don't need to set aside a special time to do this. Practice whenever you like, when you're stressed or worried, relaxed or happy. As you make it a practice to trust in inspiration, you'll find that your breath has much to say to you. Riding along on the waves of the breath will come new ideas and insights, new ways of looking at things, new ways of feeling, new ways of expressing your life, new ways of being in the world.

Practice inspirational breathing, but practice it as relaxation and as a pleasurable opening up, not as a mechanical exercise, or as work. The more you explore it, the more you will discover for yourself, the more deeply you will be able to trust it, and the more easily you will be able to move into the flow state that assists intuition.

In terms of the Intuitive Heart discovery process, following the breath is the first step because it enables you to shift gears. If you are stumped by a problem, or if you need an answer but are hindered by concern and worry, by fatigue and stress, by feelings of alienation, by getting in your own way from trying too hard, learning to make this shift can help you become more relaxed and serene. And you'll begin to see that, as that happens, ideas will flow more easily, more readily, more smoothly, and the quality of your ideas will change. As you saw with following your breath, you may feel uncertain at first, but over time that will change. You will learn how to step back and let this shift happen naturally, how to call on it when you need it, how to experience this magical combination of paying attention inwardly and, at the same time, releasing and being able to watch the flow. Or as Edgar Cayce, who was capable of bringing from within himself great knowledge and wisdom simply by relaxing and going inside himself, once said, "Learn how to watch yourself go by."

As you enter the flow, you are well on your way to understanding the secret of the Intuitive Heart, that something you have taken for granted, such as your breath, actually carries with it mystery and magic. Yet, you've been breathing all this time without thinking about it. You'll also find that you've been intuitive all along without knowing it, and that you can be intuitive intentionally, once you come to understand it and appreciate its secrets.

Trusting inspiration is a major accomplishment. It is a milestone in your ability to learn to do intentionally something you usually do naturally and unconsciously. It's a lesson you probably didn't learn in kindergarten, but it is something you can learn now from within yourself instead. With your understanding, you can harvest such moments, bring them together into a more focused, intentional awareness. Each time you practice this mindfulness and acceptance of breathing, you'll learn a little more. Your breath will bring to you ideas and notions that you'll be able to flesh out into your own intuitive messages, your own understanding, of what it means to be in the flow and of your inner wisdom.

There are a couple of ways you can practice this discovery process with the flow of your breath. One is to reread this chapter, using it as a guide through the experience of the breath; a guide that will walk you through the various levels of learning how to trust in inspiration, how those levels feel, and the higher wisdom they invoke. The second is just to practice it on your own, allowing your breath to bring whatever it will, to trust what comes. Either way, your practice will carry you naturally to intuition's next lesson, the lesson of it's higher, symbolic, spiritual significance.

Now that you no longer are taking your breath—and all that it brings—for granted, you probably will realize that there is a lot for which to be grateful within a simple breath. I'm going to show you how to follow that gratitude and how to watch it carry you along to the next level of the Intuitive Heart.

5

Step Two:
Make the Heart Connection—
Feel for Intuition

"That which cometh from the heart will go to the heart."
Jeremiah Burroughs, *In Hosea*

*M*ary was frustrated, even depressed, about her new boss, Celeste. She didn't like Celeste's style. Mary felt hostile toward Celeste's new proposals and the tasks she was giving Mary to do. So it frightened Mary the first time she was called into Celeste's office. Mary worried that her anger would show and that she would be in trouble because of her difficulty in dealing with her feelings about Celeste.

Mary decided to apply the Intuitive Heart discovery process to the situation. She followed the ritual, and when it came time to take the step of making the heart connection with the focus of her exploration, she followed her heart right into Celeste's heart. She began to experience Celeste's fear of her new job. She could see how Celeste brought good intentions with her, but felt overwhelmed by her responsibilities. Mary realized how Celeste was trying to cope by assuming a take-charge attitude.

As Mary withdrew from the experience, she noticed that her anger toward her boss was gone. In its place was compassion for Celeste and even a sense of kinship. She smiled to herself and thought, in surprise, "I know how she feels!"

The next time Mary was called into Celeste's office, Mary astonished herself by saying, "Celeste, I was just remembering when I first became a Den Mother for my son's Cub Scout program, and I always felt this pressure to make a bunch of cookies that they would really like. Do you know what it feels like to have to bake *really* good cookies?"

Celeste, too, was surprised by the question. Then she sighed in apparent relief and replied, "Yes, I do. I feel tremendous pressure right now to get cooking. Can you help me?"

From then on, Mary and Celeste worked as colleagues.

Heart Awareness Is a Mood Enhancer

"A merry heart doeth good like a medicine."   Proverbs 17:22

I'm sure you've had the experience of days when nothing seemed to go right, when everything seemed to be wrong or jinxed. I certainly have. Everything feels out of

TODAY!

kilter, and then I may get a piece of bad news, or something isn't working the way it's supposed to, or I can't get my writing to flow, or there's something I need and I can't find it. When I find myself in one of those days, I feel really low and depressed.

Then there are those other days, when things just seem to move along and everything works out. I meet with just the right people. I get good news. I seem to lead a charmed life. I'm sure you've had these experiences yourself. Such days of flow and harmony when you can't seem to take a wrong step are really special.

What I have discovered over the course of my life is that I can break the negative mindset, the feeling of being out of step, and move it toward one of being more in harmony. All I have to do is focus on the here and now. Usually, just by looking around my environment, and by taking notice of what's happening in that moment, I can change my outlook. If I can take the here and now into my heart, and find a reason to feel gratitude for what I'm experiencing at that moment, my mood gets even better. The way things go improves as well.

Sometimes I do it by finding something around me that's pleasing to look at. Sometimes I do it by coming upon some small realization, like finding something I can be grateful about. Sometimes the change comes simply from my noticing how I am free to be aware of whatever I choose at that moment, which I find entertaining and amusing. However I come by this reorientation into the pleasure of the moment, I begin to feel better, and things start to go better. I've found a way to enter the harmony of the moment, and I'm in the flow again.

Given this discovery, I find that it's hard to stay in the dark mindset for too long. I know I can change if I'm willing. It has become one of my personal challenges to learn how to stay more in the moment over longer periods of time. I'm learning to shift gears and break the spell of discord.

This ability to be in the moment, in the now, is an important factor in the experience of flow. We know that being in flow is a rewarding experience. As we used to say, being in flow is being "where it's at!" Earlier, you learned that by consciously experiencing the flow of your breath, you could change your frame of mind. You could gain a sense of wonder at the mystery of where the breath comes from, of the life force, of the inner and the outer, and start to feel connected with a larger picture. Perhaps you also discovered that those feelings have a domino effect, building and growing. The positive benefits of those feelings expand. The sense of being part of a larger whole, of being in harmony with that whole, opens us up to the source of our intuition, our unity with all life. When we are identified with the whole, we can know about the world around us without knowing how or why we know. Everything we need to know can be found within us.

One of my own earliest experiences with this wonderful mystery came while singing the "Hallelujah Chorus" in church. In the midst of that singing, chills ran up and down my spine, tears came to my eyes, and I felt a profound sense of release. I felt the release of my concerns and a positive energy in my soul, as if the Heavens had opened to me and everything was as it should be. I felt that I was a valuable person with something to do in life. I felt reborn and regenerated, as if I were getting a fresh start in life. It was like a gift coming to me, and I felt some wonderful light coming down out of the sky. In singing that lovely music, I was able to move into harmony, into flow with the music and with the other singers. I released and opened up to something bigger than myself.

Something very similar takes place as people learn about and explore the Intuitive Heart discovery process. First, the focus on the breath, especially on accepting the flow of that breath, accepting it as a gift, naturally brings a feeling of peace, and then of gratitude. People often find themselves getting images or sensations of being rocked by the breath, as if somehow life is taking care of them, and their mood begins to shift, from tension to relaxation and trust. Becoming attuned to the flow of the breath places them in harmony with the movement of their chest and their breathing. With the coming of feelings of gratitude, the sense of harmony expands beyond the body. Feelings of appreciation extend to all that is here and now, for the experience of life itself. It is this encounter with unconditional love that creates such a profound shift in how we experience ourselves. We become more "heart-centered." This popular metaphor means that we experience the world from a feeling place of love and acceptance. It also means a shift in the center of gravity, in terms of consciousness, from the head, where we experience our thoughts, down into the chest, where the heart is and where we experience love.

People notice the difference and enjoy this shift of attention into the heart area. What they tell me is that they notice a warmth, a glow, a softening of emotions, a love feeling. I have heard it described as being like the sun shining, radiating warmth, or like a rose opening, expanding and giving of itself. Others have imagined a window or door opening to the outside. What all the images have in common is warmth, radiating and expanding, and peaceful happiness.

If a person stays with this experience, to see how it may grow or develop, they tell me that the shift expands throughout their bodies and awareness. They feel like channels for the life force, feel it flowing through them, and somehow, through the intensifying of the feeling of love, the force gets brighter and brighter.

William Blake, the mystic poet, once said that gratitude is Heaven itself. This secret is a very simple way to feel good, even if just for a few moments. You might enjoy testing this idea to see if Blake was correct. If he was right, you can follow your Intuitive Heart into a very special place.

Heart Awareness Raises Consciousness

"He who harbors in his heart love of truth will live and not die."
Walter Henry Nelson, *Buddha: His Life and Teachings*

Are we talking about anything more than an improvement in mood? Well, for one thing, there is a definite physical effect to this shift. At the Institute of HeartMath® in Boulder Creek, California, a nonprofit organization devoted to exploring the ramifications of heart awareness, researchers have conducted studies on the heart's electrophysiology as it is affected by attitudes and emotions.

Their studies show that when a person focuses on the heart while experiencing appreciation and gratitude, the heart responds in kind. Its rhythm becomes more regular. An EKG taken during this time shows less noise and more regularity in the heart's electrical patterns. What's more, the brain follows along. The test subject's brain waves become more in synch and show evidence of being tuned to the heart.

The institute's discovery also is significant for our understanding of intuition experiences and of how to have a more intentional relationship with our intuition.

When we want to use our intuition, we need to quiet the mind. It's hard enough to quiet the mind under ordinary circumstances. Trying to force the mind to be quiet when we are upset is impossible. But while the brain can't quiet itself, the heart can do the job.

The Institute of HeartMath's discovery also helps us to appreciate the effects of feeling connected and in harmony with the whole. Our awareness of the breath and feelings of being in harmony with its flow helps us to experience the breath as a gift, which in turn helps us to experience gratitude for the breath, which in turn helps us to experience love in our hearts, which in turn shifts us into a higher level of order, of harmony.

Love is an experience of harmony, in which we accept things as they are, appreciate them as they are, and feel our connections with the people and world around us. Certainly, it's just common sense that if all people were more loving in this way, we would live in a more harmonious world.

The institute's research is an external, mechanical verification of something that we can experience within ourselves. It is something from which we can profit by understanding it intuitively. When we say that love is a higher state of consciousness, most of us recognize the truth of that. But what do we actually mean by it? Let's allow our intuition to teach us.

Love Is a Higher State of Consciousness

"Create in me a clean heart, O God; and renew a right spirit within me."   Psalms 51:10

I've enjoyed asking people I meet in my work to explain what is meant by "higher consciousness." It's fun to watch them grapple with something they take for granted. Often, they describe it as a wiser state of consciousness. Why then, I ask, don't we just call it wiser?

What's the wisdom in calling it higher? The response I often get is that it's not centered in the lower emotions but in the higher emotions, that love is a higher emotion than, for example, greed. That's certainly true. One of our difficulties in learning to trust intuition is getting past our concern that we are hearing our own hopes and fears and not a larger truth. It is the lower emotions that often lead us into those hopes and fears, while the higher emotion of love is identified with a broader, more noble truth. And that's very important. But, I ask again, why do we call it higher?

The answer is that, once again, we are speaking in metaphor, the language of the heart. We say "higher" because that word draws on our memories and experiences of the effect that height has on our perception. When we go to the top of a tall building or mountain, when we fly in an airplane, or any time that we physically are at a higher elevation, we can look down and see things from a new perspective. We see better how things fit together. When we are down on the ground in our little house, our awareness is of our yard and where it touches the yard of our next-door neighbor; ours is a very personal and narrow point of view. But at an elevation, we see how our house and our neighbors' houses and our whole street fit into a larger neighborhood, into a city, into an even larger geography. We get a more holistic point of view. So higher actually is a very good word-picture to describe the more encompassing consciousness that takes in more information, that has greater intelligence and a more integrated awareness of how things fit together.

Reaching Out with Our Hearts to
Understand this Metaphor of Intuitive Intimacy

"My favored temple is an humble heart."
P.J. Bailey, *Festus: Colonnade and Lawn*

Now what does love have to do with intuition? To show
you how much of a relationship there is between the
heart and the kind of thinking that deserves a label such
as "higher" to describe a quality of consciousness, let's
look again at what we mean when we talk about reaching out with the heart.

When Olympic gymnast Kerri Strug competed through
the pain of an injured ankle to help her team win a gold
medal in 1996, people agreed that their hearts "went out
to her." What does that mean? I've asked many people to
explain that expression to me. The most common answer I get is that they *cared* about her. Then why not simply say you cared? What's the wisdom in saying *your
heart went out* to her? In response to my probing, people
talk about feeling that they understood and identified
with Strug's experience. They say they had empathy for
her, could feel the way she must have felt. They were involved in and connected with what she was experiencing. It was a riveting experience, and their feelings were
united with Kerri's.

A similar phrase that we often hear, particularly when
people are married, is of two hearts being joined. People
don't actually cut open their chests and stick their hearts
together, of course, so what are we talking about? What
we mean is that the two people have a feeling, through
love, of being connected emotionally. They have a special *bond* (Here we have another metaphor, a word-picture expressing a special connection), which is to say
they share a special understanding with each other. They

are in sympathy, in *harmony* (Still another word-picture. Are they really singing?). In other words, they feel *close.* That word "close" is one more word-picture. It's hard to get away from these metaphors to describe the experience of two people sharing one act of feeling.

What we are doing with each of these common phrases about the heart, once again, is using metaphor. We talk about something that is hard to verbalize by describing it in more familiar terms and images that help us see it more clearly and vividly. A metaphor envisions the unfamiliar in more familiar terms. When we talk about the heart going out to someone, or when we talk about two people feeling close, we are using a metaphor of movement across space, or an experience of three-dimensional space, to describe in more familiar terms the process of our feelings becoming unified with someone else's feelings. The metaphor visualizes our experience of how our awareness shifts in space from where we are to where that other person is. We do move across that space in terms of consciousness to identify with another person.

It's important that you appreciate metaphors, because you use them naturally, and they represent your intuitive understanding of things. These particular metaphors also say something about our growing understanding of intuition. When we say our heart goes out to another person, we are saying that we know how they must feel because we have placed ourselves within them. We have become intuitive about them and their feelings. We have become intuitive about them because we have identified ourselves with them. We intuitively understand that intuition is created by the joining of hearts, by empathy.

When people say their hearts are joined, they mean that they have a *connection* that enables them to understand each other more intuitively, more intimately. The metaphor visualizes the experience of one person's feelings becoming what the other person feels. They become *close*. And what do we mean when we say two people are close? This metaphor visualizes the two people as if they are standing on the same spot, which describes what it's like when two people are participating in a shared experience. They can look at each other and say, "Yes, we are together in this experience. We're sharing it. We can feel each other's presence as being a part of this experience. We feel close." Two people who experience closeness with each other have intuitive feelings for each other's experience.

The metaphors that we use to describe intimacy reveal that we have an intuitive understanding that empathy, emotional unity, identification, and closeness enhance the flow of intuition between people.

It's understandable, then, that philosophers and people who are highly intuitive talk about intuition as coming from this type of intimacy with what is to be known. To be intuitive about something, we make ourselves one with it, become close to it and connected to it.

Imagined Unity Creates Intuitive Empathy

"Ye whose hearts are fresh and simple,
Who have faith in God and nature."
                    Henry Wadsworth Longfellow, *Hiawatha*

Albert Einstein used his imagination to help his understanding. He talked about developing his theory of relativity by imagining that he was riding on a beam of light. He used his imagination to become one with this lightbeam in order to understand what its experience must be. His imagined empathy brought him profound intuition about light and space. It proved to be more than "just" imagination.

Actors, too, speak of becoming one with their characters, enabling them to bring forth great expression about those characters. They bring expression from within themselves even when their own lives are very different from those of the characters they portray. When actress Barbara Hershey was interviewed about her work in "Portrait of a Lady," in which she played a character very unlike her previous roles (and very unlike her own personality), she said, "I really think everyone is inside us. If we're willing to look deep enough, hard enough, we can find anybody in there. That's how you learn about yourself, about humanity. That's the thrill of acting." It's also a great description of how to become intuitive about other people.

Another area in life where you can find plenty of examples of the intuitive connection of empathy that imagination brings is in sports. Take a close look at bowlers, for example. Watch as they roll the bowling ball down the lanes. It's as if they don't let go of the balls even when the balls leaves their hands. Watch how they follow the ball's progress with their whole bodies, shifting their bodies as if they can shift the ball, trying to steer the ball all the way down to the pins. You can see that they are not thinking about what they are doing but that, in their imagination, they have become one with the ball. They not only are experiencing the ball moving down the lanes, but they are using their imaginative connection with the ball to try to steer it.

Spectators at sports events have this same identification with the players. Watching an outfielder go back and reach up for a high-flying ball, the fans crook their heads back and move their arms. Watching gymnasts perform, or divers jump, the spectators move their bodies.

The word for empathy comes from the Greek *empatheia* and the German *Einfuhlung,* meaning feeling into. It originally was used to describe how spectators form empathic bonds with what they contemplate, often expressed by imitative movements.

In sports, people create within themselves what they experience from an identification, or momentary unity, with the object of their perception. It helps explain why spectator sports are so popular. People derive a vicarious satisfaction from watching, as if they themselves were on the playing field.

To take yet another example, watch people in a movie theater as their identification with characters and a situation brings them to tears. How many times have most of us experienced that kind of identification? Watching movies or other dramatic presentations draws us in. Our imagination allows us to enter into the story and participate in the events. We greatly expand the range of our experience through seeing such dramas.

This process of using the imagination to take the "other" into ourselves, where we create an empathic identification with the "other" and, thus, know it more intimately, is exactly the spirit of the Intuitive Heart discovery process. As we come to appreciate why people place such value on watching sports, we can appreciate more why the storytelling aspect of the Intuitive Heart is so powerful. It is the same when people watch movies or read novels. Their response to such stories, created through their imaginative identification, becomes part of their own experience, their own learning. When people listen to our stories, made from our own personal memories that we've chosen intuitively to share, they are affected in the same way. It is more powerful than giving advice because they make these stories their own as they imaginatively participate in them.

What stories do we wish to share? Let them be from the heart!

Making the Heart Connection

"What outward form and feature are
He guesseth but in part;
But that within is good and fair
He seeth with the heart."

Samuel Taylor Coleridge

When we can identify with another person through the higher consciousness of love, we have a basis for the highest, best, most profound understanding of that person. As you continue to explore the Intuitive Heart discovery process, you will be able to see and experience this fact for yourself.

At this point in your Intuitive Heart training, you have learned to follow your breath and to receive its gift, the gift of life. You are moving from that first step to the next step of focusing on your heart, experiencing gratitude for this gift, letting that gratitude blossom into a feeling of love.

Feelings of love in the heart area have a natural tendency to *expand*,. Expansion, or growing bigger, is how many people picture the change in their experience of their heart and of their entire body image when exploring feelings of gratitude. This change shows an increase in sensitivity to one's surroundings, as the expansion reflects a dissolving of tight and fixed boundaries of the self and a flowing into the environment.

Now, I think you will find that it's a very natural progression to let that feeling of love expand and to "reach out" with your heart, to explore, to greet, and to welcome. Just as you can imagine giving someone a hand-

shake in greeting, so too can you easily make a heart connection with whomever or about whatever you wish to
be intuitive. In terms of our training exercise, the Intuitive Heart discovery process, you reach out with your
heart to the person whose question or concern you are
going to address. You also will find that, in reaching out
with your heart, in making the heart connection, you
have established a foundation for understanding that
person.

Let me tell you how people have described the experience of this heart connection. In my teaching, for example, I ask people simply to focus on their breathing,
to move into a place of gratitude, aware of the expanding feeling of love, and then to imagine that they can include in that awareness the physical presence of the
person with whom they will be working. When I ask how
that feels, some people say they can feel a line going between their heart and that of their partner. Some feel as
if the partner's heart is beating in their own chest. Some
talk about the sensation of one of their bodies melding
into the other and of being able to feel the sensations of
the partner's body.

In my own experience, I often have this sensation in
the facial area. Even though my eyes are closed, I feel as
if I'm having my partner's facial expressions. I think I
know how it feels for my partner to hold the jaw or lips in
a particular way. Through the inner feeling of the facial
expression, I get an impression of my partner's mood.
All these sensations and images show the connection,
the identification, the union that takes place as we reach
out with our heart and connect with another.

Another example of the effect that such connection
can have on us is an experience I once had in art class.
We were going to draw a rose. First, however, our instructor told us to stand in front of the rose and then to ar-

range our body to stand like the rose, to become like the rose, to allow a part of us to open up the way the rose blossoms, to have our arms connected to our body the way the leaves were connected to the branches of the rose. Then, the instructor said, we would draw. As we followed the directions, the people in the class were astonished at what happened. Several talked about how they could almost smell the rose as they drew it. Others felt a new understanding of the rose, even of its thorns, which they no longer saw as an aggressive posture by the rose, but one of pride. The drawings that we did that day were much more expressive than our previous drawings of flowers and much more roselike in ways that were hard to put into words. But somehow, we knew, we had entered into the essence of that rose.

Edgar Cayce was a very intuitive man. By going deeply into himself, he was able to come up not only with facts, but also with ideas, medical solutions, and advice that were so accurate and efficacious, many consider him to have been the world's greatest psychic. He once said that our intuitive abilities have a special link with nature, which can teach us a great deal. To activate this link, he advised, a person should look at a rose, try to become like the rose, and see if, during that experience, the person didn't receive some special instruction from the rose, as if the rose were talking to them. It was the same prescription our intuitive art teacher gave our class. You can have this kind of intuitive experience as well, the experience of becoming one with another person or thing, through your Intuitive Heart connection.

As I ask the people I am training to describe the feeling of this heart connection in more detail, they speak of feeling as if they had known their partner for a long time, not in any specific sense of knowing facts about them, but a sense of closeness. "As if," said one participant, "they have their own music, and I was joined with that, and it was very pleasant."

Some talk about how, when they initially were given a partner, they didn't feel particularly positive about that person.

"But when I closed my eyes and made the heart connection," one woman said, "all of a sudden, I was exposed to a whole new world, and I experienced this person very differently. And they were beautiful."

"It's not just a feeling of being close," a third person explained, "but of being close to them in a way that has a certain quality, a certain sound, or aroma, or atmosphere to it."

You can see the difficulty we have, sometimes, in articulating exactly what we experience when we make this heart connection, yet most of the people in my classes always nod in agreement with such descriptions, understanding exactly what each of the speakers means when trying to describe the heart connection.

Which isn't to say that each person has exactly the same experience. In a group setting, I instruct the participants to make heart connections with more than one partner. What they notice is that each connection feels different, that each is as unique as the person sitting across from them. These connection experiences are not just some generalized experience of halos or hearts and flowers or Christmasy kinds of sweet stuff. Yet, even though each feels different, there is a common denominator in each experience: you. You can feel yourself in each one, and you can see, through the differences, the common essence that connects all these experiences.

The heart connection is real, and it has real effects. When I ask people whether they felt something real was happening as their heart connected with the other person, almost everyone agrees it felt real. How do they know it was real, I ask, since they were just sitting with their eyes closed, not touching in any ordinary physical way. It would be easy to say it was their imagination. Yet, almost to a person, they insist that the connection was real, that they could feel it, and that they "just know it."

What is happening here, of course, is that this heart connection is an intuitive experience, something that we know outside our usual ways of knowing. It's worth practicing the heart connection just to experience this moment of intuitive awareness, which you will find you trust and value. Too often, we work at having intuition while forgetting that it comes through a particular mode of experience with which many of us have little practice. In order to recognize and trust intuition, we need to spend time experiencing and appreciating this mode. And I find that it's in the practice of making heart connections that most of the people with whom I work can have that awareness, that experience of "Yes, I can see how I'm being intuitive and that the heart connection I feel with this person is real."

The sense of intuitive connection with another person is more than "just" imagination. When I ask people to help me explain to others how real it is, they often refer to the insights they've experienced into the other person during the heart connection. After a minute or so of quietly contemplating this heart connection, people have surprising insights about their partner, just as Mary did about her boss, Celeste. I remember one man, for example, who said that he sensed his partner, a young woman, had a "heavy heart," and that it reminded him of how he felt when his wife died. As it turned out, the woman had just ended a long-term relationship and also had lost her mother to death the previous month.

We can imagine a heart connection, but it becomes more than "just" imagination. Try it for yourself and see.

Learn to Trust Your Heart

"My heart is as true as steel."
William Shakespeare, *A Midsummer Night's Dream*

For now, you need to take some time to practice making the heart connection and experiencing how it feels for you and with different people and things. Each time you practice this, begin with your focus on the breath, letting the gratitude for the breath come, and letting that gratitude expand into love. When you have enjoyed that experience for a moment, then use it to reach out to another person. You don't need their permission to do this, because I don't think we need permission to feel love toward another. If the person is someone you feel comfortable asking for permission, you can have a more shared experience that can provide you with valuable feedback. In either case, notice what you experience as your gratitude, love, and heart awareness expand to include that person. Notice your attitude toward that person and whether it changes. Notice what you sense from them. Do it with several people to see how your perceptions are different and what they have in common.

You also can practice this connection with non-human objects. Flowers and trees are wonderful subjects. See how your experience of their nature changes when you make a heart connection with them.

What all of your practice will do is to help you see that the heart has a unique way of perceiving, that the heart connection is a natural form of identification and empathy, and that through this empathic response, you do have the ability for intuitive perception, for that inner connection. When you move to the final step in the Intuitive Heart training—getting feedback—it will emphasize not only your ability to have intuitive perceptions but also the reality of the connections that your Intuitive Heart is making.

You can learn to trust your heart and to follow it. Using heart awareness—love—as a means of understanding is to follow a path of harmony. When you are ready to live in a world of harmony, then you can follow your heart, for it intuitively responds to that greater world. The heart has a higher consciousness that is available to you through the experience of making heart connections

As you learn to make these heart connections, you are surrendering to love as a channel of understanding and inspiration. And just as we have used metaphors (higher consciousness, reaching out with the heart, joining hearts, a heart connection) to describe what happens, so, too, will the wisdom that comes forth from your heart be expressed in the heart's language, the language of the imagination and memory, the figures of speech and word pictures that are the language of metaphor.

This experience of the heart connection is as valuable a lesson about how intuition works as that of the breath.

You may remember that, with the breath, what made it possible to get out of your own way was to realize that your breath is inherently trustworthy. You realized that, as you watched it and began to relax about it, the breath continued to come on its own, just as it always has. You learned to trust that, even when you aren't thinking about it, the breath will go on. It's the same with the heart connection. You worry and clutch at that moment for the insight or awareness you're supposed to get. But two things help you to relax. One is the good feeling of that moment of the other person's presence, the feeling of being connected, the love feeling. The other is the experience of knowing that for that moment, love fills your heart, and love is enough. This experience of the loving connection can fill your awareness, so that there is no need for anything else. The satisfaction of that moment, the blossoming of love, the flowering of the heart connection's energy, all pour forth and displace our fretting. It's as if you stand aside and let love take over.

No doubt you've had other such moments in your life, moments when you were focusing on some issue, tense and worried, and unable to release it. Then you may have felt the nudging of love, beckoning and saying, here is the loving thing to do. And if you were able to heed that voice, to release all your worry and tension into love, to go where love would have you go, you probably were filled with a wonderful sense of relief and peace.

This kind of experience is an exercise of the Intuitive Heart and one that can support your training. Researchers at the Institute of HeartMath confirmed its effectiveness, and the institute now teaches people how to approach concerns and worrisome situations by releasing them into love. When you focus on a problem that way, the love pushes aside your concerns and brings in its wake new solutions, new approaches to the situation. We'll talk more about this a little later.

Right now, let's go on with your training. You have learned to follow your breath, to experience gratitude and love, and to expand those feelings into a connection from your heart to your partner. Now you're going to learn to allow the guidance and the information to come.

Just as you did with following the breath, where you probably were concerned at first with what you should think and do, you may be worried now about what kind of memory you should get, what kind of guidance you should receive, what sort of teaching lesson you should make. But as I showed you with the breath, what you really need to do is to relax, stop worrying about it, just enjoy the feeling of the love connection. In other words, just get out of your own way. If you can relax into this experience and enjoy it and be grateful for it, it will help take your mind off all that worry and will enable your intuition, which is love and its higher intelligence, to bring forward the inspiration you seek.

As I consider this and reach out to it from my own Intuitive Heart, it reminds me of a time when I went out on a fishing boat with a group of people. We all had paid money to go out on this boat to catch fish, so we really wanted to catch some. But no one was catching anything. We tried different kinds of bait and moved around to different spots on the water. Nothing was happening. Finally, I began to be seduced by the beauty of the day. It was sunny and warm, and the boat was rocking gently on the water. I forgot to worry about catching fish and drifted off into this wonderful state of reverie. And the next thing I remember was people shaking me and saying, "Henry, you've got a bite!"

My memory shows me that it is much the same in intuition and its heart connection. You can just let it happen. You can trust in it. You can trust the breath, the love, and the heart, and the heart will make the connection you seek.

6

Steps Three and Four:
Invite a Memory and Tell Your Story

"No calamity befalls but by the permission of God: and whoso believes in God, He will guide his heart; for God all things doth know!"

Koran

While you may think your memories have little importance to anyone except you, in fact, they can play a key role in accessing your Intuitive Heart. The technique I'll use to demonstrate this is something I call the Memory Bowl Game. It's easy to do. Just lighten up and let yourself go. Like Hanson:

Hanson, who was practicing the memory bowl technique, had been waving his hands and clapped them together just as his son, Jeffrey, walked into the room.

"Whatcha doing Dad, trying to catch a fly?"

"No, Jeffrey, I was trying to remember something."

"Oh," Jeffrey responded, curious, "did you forget something?"

"No, it's not that I've forgotten something. I'm trying to remember something I haven't ever remembered before."

Jeffrey became more curious. "What's that?"

"I don't know. I don't know what it is I'm trying to remember. I'm just trying to remember it anyway." Hanson hoped this mysterious statement would quiet his son, who had caught him in this somewhat embarrassing situation. But Jeffrey surprised him.

"You mean like Soccer Teese, Dad? We learned in school about this man Soccer Teese who said we never really learn anything, we just remember it."

"So how do you suppose you remember something," Hanson asked, "when you don't know what it is that you are trying to remember?"

"Well," said Jeffrey, "the teacher asked us that same question."

"So what is the answer?"

"I guess you just jiggle your head a little." At that, Jeffrey made a funny face worthy of Jim Carey. He jiggled his head, making his lips flap and his body shake. "And maybe the memory just pops out into your mind."

Hanson couldn't help but laugh. And as he did, he suddenly remembered something he hadn't thought of in years. It was a time his own dad had teased him. They were out fishing, and the young Hanson was working hard to put the worm on the hook just right so it wouldn't fall off. His dad came over to him and said in a very serious tone, "Be sure to put the worm on so it curves back just like a pretzel."

"Why, Dad?" Hanson had asked his own father.

"Because fish really like pretzels, even better than worms," his dad answered.

"Gee, really?" Hanson had wanted to know. Then he had seen the twinkle in his dad's eye and knew his dad was teasing him for trying too hard to put the worm on the hook *just right.*

"Lighten up!" Hanson said to his own son. "That's what I have to do!"

"What's that?" Jeffrey asked.

Hanson took a deep breath. As he let out a sigh, he jiggled his head just as Jeffrey had done, and then they both laughed together. After that, Hanson had no more trouble playing the memory game.

In fact, Hanson already had played the memory game, with his memory of the pretzel worms, without even realizing it.

What's the First Thing that Pops into Your Head?

"I hear it in the deep heart's core."
                William Butler Yeats, *The Lake Isle of Innisfree*

Learning to be intuitive is learning how to get into a natural flow. Like the graceful flow of the champion athlete, who makes all the right moves, your natural intuition brings you to the right places at the right times. Like your breath, that brings inspiration to you just as you need it, your natural intuition can bring just the right thoughts and insights to mind at the right moment, right when you need them. Can you learn to trust the flow of your thoughts just as you are learning to trust the flow of your breath? Of course you can. As you continue to explore the steps and layers of the Intuitive Heart discovery process, you are going to learn just how much you *can* trust inspiration.

Your intuitive thoughts are just a breath away. A key step in the Intuitive Heart process, as you saw in chapter 2, is inviting a memory to come into the mind. It's as if you're receiving the seed of intuition's wisdom.

You probably are wondering, why a memory? It's a good question and one we'll answer later. But first, let's explore the process of allowing a memory to pop into your mind.

You've learned how to become aware of and enter into the flow of your breath. The breath carries surprising significance. Now, you're going to learn how to let helpful memories flow spontaneously into your mind and how to understand their significance. And because the natural tendency is to question and influence your choice of memories, just as you did with your breath, I'll show you how to get past that tendency, how to let the memories come on their own.

To illustrate the challenge, I ask people if they have memories. Yes, everyone says, they do. Okay, I say, then just be spontaneous and have a memory. And immediately people either smile or look confused. There's nothing more natural than recalling memories, but as soon as I call attention to the process, everyone becomes very self-conscious about it. They want to know what memory they are supposed to recall. They want to know what would be the best memory to remember. If they recall a memory, they question whether or not it's a meaningful memory, or a real memory, or if it's complete. And sometimes a person suddenly can't think of a single memory at all. To help people past this stumbling block of self-awareness, I give them specific things to remember: how

their back yard looks, a neighbor, a former teacher, etc.
Then, of course, they are able to remember something.

Clearly, I tell them, people are able to pull down a
memory when they know in advance what they're going
after. But the big question is how to allow a memory to
pop up on its own, how to get past that need to screen
and select, that need to second-guess which memory
should appear.

When I teach people how to let memories come on
their own, I play the Memory Bowl Game. You can play
it, too. The game is to pretend that all your memories,
the millions and millions of momentary experiences
you've ever had, are like a bunch of ping pong balls or
marbles in a giant spherical bowl, like the bowls used in
state lottery drawings. All your memories, big and small,
significant and insignificant, traumatic and pleasant,
even neutral and trivial, are all little balls in this giant
bowl. Now, imagine shaking and rolling this big memory
bowl around and around. It's best to stick out your arms
and wave them around and around, the way a football
umpire might in giving some signal, but you're imagining that you are rolling this large memory bowl. After
you've rolled the bowl around three times, bring your
arms together and clap your hands. At the clap of your
hands, let yourself be surprised by the first memory that
comes to mind.

When I demonstrate this little game in front of audi-
ences, I really ham it up to get people in the mood to
loosen up and play. I twirl my arms in giant circles, and I
make a funny runaway siren sound with my mouth to
suggest that things are getting way out of control. Then
the sound reaches an exhilarated peak, and I clap my
hands. People are surprised, and most everyone has a
memory jolted loose.

Picturing the bowl full of memories distracts that rational, questioning part of the brain long enough for a spontaneous memory to surface. Waving the arms around, making the funny noises, making it like a game, are all little things that help your mind loosen up, that help you let go of control and stop worrying about what memory should appear. Loosening up the mind, just as Jeffrey taught his father by rattling his head and rippling his face, is also a humorous way to let a little chaos help create greater flexibility and openness to novel memories that are more responsive to intuition and subtle promptings.

The best way for you to see how it works is to try it for yourself. Again, because learning a new technique requires some concentration, it may feel a little awkward. Just let yourself relax into it as much as possible and work with whatever comes. If you're alone or in a comfortable situation, you may want to make a circle with your arms as you stir the memory bowl, to help distract you from too much thought about what memory might come to you. If not, you can try visualizing the memory bowl and its spinning in your mind. Again, its purpose is to turn off that editor in your brain that questions everything, turn it off in order to access the often-subtle images that are the basis for the work of the Intuitive Heart.

I find that, more often than not, people have a memory appear on the first try. If you don't, then spin the memory bowl again to let a memory come to the surface when you clap your hands together. Once you are familiar with the process, it's easy to make a game of it, spinning the arms, clapping the hands, making faces and noises if you want, and having a memory appear at the clap of the hands.

Some memories are more familiar, some less so. It doesn't really matter at this point, as the main goal of the game is to let it become more comfortable to accept that memories can pop up to the surface of the mind. Later, as you go along, you can see how often you can surprise yourself by recalling memories that you haven't remembered in a long time. It's fun to see what pops up. Some of the memories are really surprising, taking you to people and places you had totally forgotten. The process becomes almost like dreaming, where someone way out of your past makes a surprise appearance. It makes you wonder why you would think of that person, place or event. That kind of wondering will lead you right into a deeper intuitive appreciation for the discovery process I'm teaching you here, because, just as in a dream, a memory can be used as the seed for a story that brings wisdom.

As you learn to use this game to receive random memories, you gradually can eliminate the outward arm movements and hand clapping. You can do it all in your imagination. Just picture your mind spinning about, and cluck your tongue and see what memory comes. Always go with the first memory or fragment that pops into your mind, no matter how trivial or out of context it may seem to be. I also should mention here that, sometimes, the memory may be something very subtle: a bodily sensation, perhaps, or a brief flash of a picture. Tune in to whatever you get, and build upon it. Ask yourself what it reminds you of, what else comes to mind, and generally, you'll find a specific memory appearing. As you accept and explore what comes, regardless of its initial appearance, it becomes progressively easier to get out of your own way and to let the memories come on their own.

Memories Are What Stories Are Made From

"Tell me where is fancy bred,
Or in the heart or in the head?"
                    William Shakespeare, *The Merchant of Venice*

When you're comfortable that a memory will come when you ask for one, you'll be ready for the next step. You can take the memory and use it as a starting point to tell a story. Simply use your memory to tell a story. That's about as natural and simple as telling someone the memory itself, because it's only natural to explain what was happening at the time of the experience that created that memory. We all naturally tell stories when we tell people what happened to us.

For example, as I'm writing this material, I stepped aside and played the memory bowl game myself. I asked for a memory that I could use to illustrate for you how we can tell a story from a memory. What came to me is a memory of a time when I went out to sweep up the leaves and other things along the sidewalk at my house, and I couldn't find the broom:

> I was outside in the yard looking around for my broom. I couldn't find it in any of the places I usually leave it. Then I happened to see my neighbor's broom in his yard. So I went over and borrowed it for my own use. I used it to sweep my sidewalk. I remember how different that broom felt from my own. Mine was the flat broom you sweep from side to side, and his was a push broom that you move along in front of you. As I used his broom, I was thinking about what it would be like to get a new broom and use a different kind of broom to sweep. When I was done, I took the broom back to my

neighbor's house and replaced it exactly as I had found it. I suspected that he would be none the wiser that I had used it. For myself, however, I had gained a new perspective on sweeping.

There. I've made a story from my memory.

I think you will agree with me that it wasn't a really profound story, but neither was it too difficult to retrieve or tell. I simply told you what happened. It naturally came out as a story. It seems like a pretty trivial memory to start with. But that's okay. We need to learn not to judge what comes to us when we invite our intuition to speak. We need to learn to trust the memory that comes and how to turn it into a story. The story honors the memory and brings it to life. We'll see in the next chapter how to use this story as a seed for wisdom. In chapter 6, we'll look more closely at how to take the memory you get and understand the wisdom of what your Intuitive Heart is saying. But we want to take this a step at a time. First, let's do some further exploration of the process of getting a memory and telling its story.

Try it now yourself. Start with your hands in front of you, a few inches apart, and then rotate your arms around in large circles, three times. And as you do this, or if you are just visualizing, imagine the Memory Bowl spinning all your memories around. Wiggle your head a little, if you want, to help loosen you up physically and mentally. At the clap of your hands, imagine putting in your hand and pulling out a memory or imagine that a lottery ping-pong ball pops out with a memory for you. Look at your memory and accept the first thing that comes into your mind, no matter how subtle or trivial. And now, you're going to take that memory, whatever it is, and turn it into a story.

I'm going to do it again myself. This time, what I get is

being aware of a tension in my right shoulder. I focus on that sensation a little and soon it reminds me of carrying a log on my shoulder:

> I remember once, when I was a teenager, my dad was working out in back of the house, building a patio. I was standing around watching, wondering at the skills and know-how he had learned about building things. I asked him if I could help, but I didn't think that there was really anything I could do. As expected, he said not right then but that, maybe later, I could.
>
> I went back inside to my room, where my attention soon was caught by my closet and all the stuff in it. I decided to clean it out. I was pulling all this stuff out and putting it in big plastic bags. This one bag was filled with magazines that I had kept for years, but finally I was able to stuff them all in. I bent over to lift the bags, and the magazines were very unruly; they all kept moving and sliding this way and that. Eventually, I had to clutch the bag by the top and lift it over my shoulder like Santa Claus. Using one hand to open the door and the other to clutch the bag, I finally made it outside and down the sidewalk to the garbage cans. Then I had to heave the bag up off my shoulder (Oh, did that hurt!) to get it into the can. And I said good riddance to the magazines that had taken up my closet space for so long.
>
> Then my dad came out front to where I was and pointed to the pile of lumber that had been delivered. He asked me to help him carry this big beam. It was at least six inches thick, or more, and just as wide. It was as heavy as a log. He showed me how to carefully squat down, and then to lift the beam and

put it on our shoulders. We slowly stood up and walked the beam to the back yard. My shoulder was already a bit sore, but it felt good to be helping my dad, and it was more fun than cleaning out the closet.

That's my memory and its story. I've taken a small sensation that came into my awareness and, as I focused in on it, it got elaborated into a particular moment, and that moment into a story. The memory didn't sound like much, just the memory of a physical sensation. But there was, in fact, a story there after all.

If you can learn to quiet your mind and trust in your memories, you can play this game. You can allow yourself to be surprised by a memory that comes to you and then turn it into a story.

Talking the memory out, either with someone else or by yourself, can be very conducive to developing your story. If you are practicing this alone, you may want to try talking into a tape recorder or even writing down your memory and your thoughts about it. The key is just to accept the memory. By embracing it, you give it energy, and this can help you focus on it.

As you practice this game, or even just think about it, you may have some doubts as to its value. The memories may not seem significant. The stories would not be best sellers. Maybe it feels to you as if you're not really doing anything. In fact, it may feel like you're just making it all up as you go along. Shouldn't intuition—and its stories—just appear to you, you may ask. Why should you have to make an effort?

Those questions are valid and understandable, especially since you may not be sure if you believe you really can be intuitive. I've heard all these questions before. There are many ways to address these concerns. One way is to ask you to wait until you are doing the entire Intuitive Heart discovery process to help someone who is dealing with a real problem. Then you'll experience the value of this step of the training. Another way I can help is to tell you a true story.

What Begins as Pretending Can Become Surprisingly Real

"I am certain of nothing but of the holiness of the heart's affections, and the truth of Imagination. What the Imagination seizes as Beauty must be Truth, whether it existed before or not."

John Keats, *Letters*

A group of hypnosis researchers found an interesting effect in one of their projects that I think is similar to what is happening as you retrieve your memories and tell your stories. These researchers were trying to understand why some people could not be hypnotized while others seem to do it effortlessly. They talked to the subjects in each group, asking them to describe what it felt like as they listened to the hypnotist's suggestions and as they moved into a hypnotic state. The most striking difference between the two groups was the ability of the people who could be hypnotized to listen to the hypnotic suggestions with an attitude of "Why not? Sure, I can imagine that I'm doing that." The people who had difficulty being hypnotized, on the other hand, would say, "Okay, let's see. Let's see if my arms really do feel heavy." They mentally stood behind a barrier of skepticism and passivity, doing nothing and waiting for the hypnotic trance to come along and seize them. The successful subjects, in effect, agreed to help the hypnotist out by playing along.

Then the researchers decided to see what happened if

they trained the unhypnotizable subjects to act more like their counterparts. "We want you to pretend," the researchers told them. "Just imagine what it would feel like if you were being hypnotized. Go along with it. Pretend it's happening."

The results were significant. Many of these "unhypnotizable" people found that, although they started out pretending, they soon found themselves so involved that they were following the hypnotist's suggestions even before they could pretend to do so. In fact, they had been hypnotized after all. It was the suggestion that they pretend that helped them get past the mental posture that had been freezing them in their tracks.

The Memory Bowl game is the same way. If you think that nothing is coming to you, chances are you are getting caught up in the idea that nothing useful will come, or that things actually are coming to you but you're dismissing them as not being what we're looking for. So trust that the memories will come. Step out of your own way to let it happen. Then practice, because it's the best way to experience how your own memories come. Finally, you tell a story from the memory, because it's a natural, easy thing to do.

Why Memories?

"We know truth, not only by reason, but also by the heart, and it is from this last that we know first principles; and reason, which has nothing to do with it, tries in vain to combat them. The skeptics who desire truth alone labor in vain."   Blaise Pascal, *Pensees No. 4*

When Claire Sylvia received a heart-lung transplant, she received an unexpected bonus. She had dreams of the person whose heart and lungs were now part of her new life. She also experienced changes in her tastes, style of dancing, and other details of her mode of being that suggested she had taken on some of the characteristics of the donor. In her book, *A Change of Heart,* she describes the puzzlement, surprise, and amazing new outlook that this transformation meant to her.

The heart seems to have the ability to store memories. We usually think of our memories as stored in our head, or brain, but there is good evidence that the heart has an important role in how we learn from experience. In his book, *The Heart's Code: Tapping the Wisdom and Power of Our Heart Energy,* psychologist Paul Pearsall, Ph.D., reviews the evidence for the role of the heart in cellular memories and how they provide the bridge that connects spirit, mind, and body. What we have been experiencing here in our Intuitive Heart discovery process, following a purely intuitively approach, is proving scientifically to have a physiological basis. The heart seems to hold a more important key to our health, happiness and wisdom than we would have previously suspected, and its ability to hold memories is one of its important duties. We talk about "knowing it by heart," when our knowledge is simply a part of who we are. It gives us a clue about the relationship between experience and intuition. Nursing research has confirmed this longstanding conventional wisdom.

The nursing profession is ahead of the game. Nurses know what it really takes to heal. They are the ones who are present with the patients, spending time with them, listening to their complaints, tending to their needs. It is nurses who have put into words the intuitive wisdom that it is *caring* that is helpful, not just the medical technology. It is nurses who have developed the understanding of what caring is all about. Nurses recognize further that caring requires *intuition.* You'll not find mention of intuition in the textbooks that doctors use, at least not yet. But intuition *is* part of the standards of practice for many nurses. The American Association of Holistic Nurses officially recognizes intuition and puts it into print.

It is nursing research that has confirmed another intuition about intuition. One survey, for example, showed that it is the older, more experienced nurses who most readily trust their intuition and use it on the job. In this recognition, they are echoing some common wisdom about how intuition operates. It often draws upon experience. It uses the little cues in a situation, cues the conscious mind doesn't even notice, to alert the right wisdom, based upon a wealth of past experience.

In its simplest form, intuition draws upon memory as a natural resource. It's one of the reasons I emphasize learning how to allow memories to come to you as the starting point for your intuition. But there's more.

It might seem that you should give intuition free rein. What if the first thing that comes to mind is an image or a thought, not a memory? Why shouldn't you accept the first thing that comes, no matter what it is, even if it is not a memory? Ultimately, that rule of thumb will be quite helpful, but not necessarily at this beginning stage of our work. Here's why:

Intuitions come from within us. It's easy to accept, when you are just beginning, that memories come from within you, even when you are not quite sure that the particular memory is very meaningful. But it would be a lot harder to establish a relationship with a bizarre image that just pops into our mind. Such images might seem to have no connection with you. You probably soon would assume that these images represented some form of "psychic perception" about someone or something "out there." It would change your relationship to your intuition, making it more mysterious and alienating you from it. Before the end of this book, you will learn to accept and find meaning in both images and in all other kinds of experiences that come your way when you invoke intuition. But for the time being, as you are learning, if you can "find it in your heart" to understand the meaning of the memories that come your way, you'll be off to a good start.

Telling a story is a good way to expand upon the meaning of a memory or experience. It is easier, and more natural, to expand upon your own memories than upon some image that may seem foreign to you. Your memories are the seeds of actual stories. Since the memories belong to you, it's easy to tell the story of what happened to you, of how that memory came to be. It's also easier to learn from stories. It may be hard to extract wisdom from an alien image, but it is relatively easy to find the wisdom that experience teaches you when you are dealing with one of your own memories.

With a little practice, you'll find that receiving a memory and telling a story about it are not difficult to do. You are a born storyteller. We all are. And, as with every other step in opening your Intuitive Heart, you are doing what comes naturally. Now, let's talk about the intuitive wisdom hidden in those stories.

7

Step Five:
Searching Your Heart for Wisdom—
Making Metaphors from Memories

"The heart is wiser than the intellect."   J.G. Holland, *Kathrina*

When we want to understand something, we can ask two different questions.

We can ask, "How does it work?"

Or we can ask, "What's the story?"

There's a very important difference between an explanation and a story. An explanation will analyze, dissect, show principles, rules, or laws. But a story touches us. It can excite us and move us. It can shape our awareness in a way that an explanation can't. We stand back and examine an explanation. We participate in a story and learn directly from our vicarious experience. Let me show you what I mean:

When Rachel appeared at work one morning with a tear-stained face, it was clear that something was seriously wrong. Matthew asked if he could help, but Rachel said she didn't see how, since her marriage counselor so far hadn't been able to. Rachel said she was very unhappy in her marriage. But, she said, her husband was a decent guy, and she was wracked with guilt that she was considering leaving him.

"Making that decision can be tough," Matthew told her, "but sometimes you just have to make the break so everyone can get on with their lives and be happier in the long run."

Rachel gave Matthew a bleak look and went to her office, clearly not particularly helped by his blunt advice.

Two weeks later, she looked more grim than ever.

"No progress on the home front?" Matthew asked. He had been unable to stop thinking about how upset Rachel had been looking. At her negative shake of the head, Matthew felt his heart go out to her in her pain. Sincerely wanting to help, he went back to his office and went through the steps of the Intuitive Heart discovery process, which he had learned at a seminar the previous weekend. A few minutes later, he stood at Rachel's office door.

"You know," Matthew said, "seeing how sad you are reminded me of the time, when I was twelve years old and my brother wanted to leave home. My father had died three years before, and my mother came to rely heavily on my brother, who was seven years older than I was. Now, he wanted to go to college. In fact, he already had postponed going for a year because it upset my mom so much. But he was miserable staying there, and that meant none of us was really happy."

Matthew said his brother finally made the decision to go anyway.

"My mom cried for a while," he said, "but eventually, it got easier. Before long, she started volunteering at the hospital, and she even got a part-time job. She was like a different person. It was because my brother finally made the hard decision he knew he had to make for his own future that turned out to be the biggest favor he could do for all of us."

At Matthew's story, Rachel's face looked peaceful for the first time in weeks, and she smiled at him through her tears.

"Thank you, Matthew," she said. "That's just what I've needed to hear. The problem is that I realized I really don't love my husband, that I married him to make my family and his happy, but it was a mistake. I haven't been able to bring myself to leave because he does love me, and I don't want to hurt him. Your story just made me see that I'm hurting him anyway, by staying when I'm so unhappy and don't love him. I just realized that I will hurt him less by ending things now so we both can go on to happier lives."

Matthew's heartfelt, intuitive story did for Rachel what his sensible, straightforward advice could not do.

Today, there are any number of psychologists and anthropologists looking at what it is about stories that is so important to humans. Before we had explanations, we had stories. Stories are more rudimentary, more permanent, and touch us at a deeper level. Explanations came with the development of science and philosophy, in which we work with certain abstract rules: the laws of nature and the principles of philosophy. Stories deal, instead, with truths and are much more complex and rich. When you work in a storytelling mode, you draw from within, from a rich source of energy, enthusiasm, feelings, wisdom, and understanding. An explanation, on the other hand, is distant, superficial, even glib. Its energy level is much lower. Working from your Intuitive Heart, you'll find that stories lend themselves most naturally to that process. ⨻

Exploring What Stories Have to Teach Us

"So teach us to number our days, that we may apply our hearts unto wisdom."   Psalms 90:12

Once you have retrieved a memory and spun a story from it, then you are ready to explore the intuitive power hidden there. You can use that power to provide guidance and wisdom.

Recall the broom memory I described in the previous chapter. I couldn't find my broom, and so I borrowed my neighbor's broom, which was quite different from mine. Watch as I "search my heart for wisdom" and turn the memory into a teaching story.

What can I say about this memory? I don't know, but I'll just start exploring—making it up as I go. Speaking "from the heart," by which I mean sincerely, openly, and extemporaneously, without knowing in advance what may come out, I could say, for starters, that something was missing. Something I needed was not available. I looked around and saw that my neighbor had something I could use instead to accomplish my goal. What I didn't have, someone else had, and I could use it. And as I used

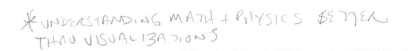

⨻ UNDERSTANDING MATH + PHYSICS BETTER
THRU VISUALIZATIONS

it, it started me thinking about making use of a different kind of tool than I was used to. Is there a message I can draw from that?

One obvious message could be that, if I don't have my usual way of dealing with something, I can look around and get an idea from someone else. I can borrow what they use, and in doing that, I can get a new handle, find a new way of approaching the situation, thus gaining new perspectives. I realize new possibilities that hadn't occurred to me before.

As I think about it more, it brings to mind situations where I'm about to deal with something I've dealt with many times before, but suddenly I'm caught short, without my usual resources. Instead, I have to draw on my environment for a substitute resource, and in the course of doing that, I find it bringing up new ideas for how to approach a task. Something that I thought at first was a "bad" and upsetting situation, I am able to remedy by turning to something else around me, and this results in an expansion of my horizons and an opening of new possibilities.

What is the lesson here? For a story to be a teaching story, it means that it has a lesson. The lesson could be that I shouldn't be afraid when I don't have my accustomed way of doing something. It can be an opportunity to borrow or adapt another way, thus adding to my own repertoire and discovering new possibilities.

It's a lesson that has particular meaning for me in the writing of this book. I didn't have the time usually necessary to get this book started. As a result, I had to open to new possibilities. Brenda English, who has practiced the Intuitive Heart work enough to teach it, agreed to help me as a co-writer. She helped me get the book off the ground, then helped me through to the end. I had never co-written a book before, and I didn't think it would be possible, especially a book about something as close and personal to me as this work. But because of my time constraints, I was willing to try something new, something that has given me an important new tool for accomplishing my goals.

Here you easily can see how I was able to take a little story I had created from a memory and, by thinking about it, was able to turn it into a teaching story with a lesson. I brought other memories and wisdom to bear in shaping an important lesson to myself. Exactly how did I do this? I went from the story to a discussion of what the events in the story meant to me. From there, I explored what lessons I drew from those events, both at the time of the experience and later, such as my current situation working on this book. What came to me as I went through this process was that I realized an important lesson for myself. The wisdom in this lesson is something that I can use in the future and that might be of value to someone else as well.

Metaphors: Something Old Explains Something New

"The heart is like an instrument whose strings
Steal nobler music from Life's many frets."

Gerald Massey, *Wedded Love*

In my example, I was working with a memory story about a broom, but the wisdom wasn't about getting a different broom. The broom was a metaphor for a tool I was accustomed to having available. Likewise, the neighbor wasn't just a neighbor but also a metaphor for resources in my nearby environment, resources that weren't necessarily those to which I was accustomed, but resources that I could borrow and use. In discovering the wisdom in the story, I wasn't talking merely about sweeping the sidewalk (who needs a lot of wisdom about that?) but about how to get my tasks done, or more generally, how to accomplish goals. My memory was transformed into a metaphor to teach me something significant about my life.

A metaphor is a word picture. You make a metaphor by using a more familiar word or concept to picture something else that is less familiar and more difficult to put into words. For example, we can use a rose as a metaphor to picture love by saying that "love is a rose." In this metaphor, we are using the word picture to help us see the rose-like qualities of love: the opening up and blossoming; perhaps in the case of romantic love, even the tendency to fade after a short but intense time of beauty.

The heart is often used to make metaphors. We've already mentioned the one where we say our heart "goes out" to somebody as a means of picturing what happens in moments of compassion. With the exception of Jim Carey's animated heart in *The Mask,* none of us has ever seen a heart actually going out from one person to another. But we know the feeling described. It is hard to put into words the strange experience that happens in moments of compassion. We use the phrase "heart goes out" to create a picture of our heart feelings moving in space to be physically close to someone. The image helps us to picture what is otherwise difficult to conceive and even more difficult to describe in words. The subjective qualities of intense empathy sometimes involve an experience that seems as if our center of feeling shifts to be close to, or actually within, the other person. An event that is hard to see becomes more "visible" and understandable when it is "viewed" by using the word picture provided by the metaphor of the heart going out.

A metaphor is a tool for understanding. We use our understanding of something more familiar to provide a model to help us understand something new or strange to us. Using metaphors is a basic way humans have for creating understanding and exploring new territory. Scientists, for example, for a long time used their understanding of the solar system to picture the structure of the atom. They envisioned several planetary electrons revolving around a central nucleus like the sun. Exploring the implications of that model helped them go beyond it to still greater understanding. Knowledge is a growing thing.

Using metaphors to probe the unknown is exactly what we do in the Intuitive Heart method. We allow a memory to come, and then the memory's expanded story contains emotions and dynamics that are used as metaphors to help us understand another situation that is more or less unknown. The Intuitive Heart discovery process has its roots in a very ancient and universal method of exploring the unknown.

In order to help people relax and trust their natural abilities, I turn my training in the Intuitive Heart method into something like a game. But it is far more than just a game. The Intuitive Heart has lofty goals. One goal, of course, is to learn how to tap a deep source of wisdom that's within us all. A second goal is to use the process itself as a working metaphor to help us gain a better understanding of the mysteries of intuition.

Intuition brings new understanding and guidance because metaphors reveal new patterns and ways of seeing. When you let a memory become a teaching story, metaphor gives you a new way of looking at things. The story and its wisdom, its metaphors, give you a way of understanding that links into your own experience. As you tell your stories and then search for the metaphors of their wisdom, what you are doing is learning to see with the heart.

It Takes Imagination to See with the Heart

It is only with the heart that one can see rightly; what is essential is
invisible to the eye.   Antoine de Saint-Exupery

What does it mean to see with the heart? Obviously,
the heart has no eyes, so how can a heart see? Once
again, we are using metaphor. We use what we already
understand about the eyes to explore our still-dim understanding of intuition and its relationship to the heart,
which is itself a metaphor for our center of feeling. We
are picturing how the heart, by feeling, detects what is in
its environment, just as the eyes do. Seeing with the
heart means understanding by feeling, finding or exam-
ining patterns with feeling. With our eyes, we become
aware of what's around us, and by focusing and concen-
trating, we become more aware of certain kinds of information. The heart does this as well, by "seeing" with
feelings.

Often, however, these feelings are quite subtle. So how
does the heart focus those feelings for you to "see" more
clearly? The heart sees through the vehicle of imagination. The imagination can help you identify and articu-
late these often-subtle feelings, by drawing on your own
past experiences as metaphors for a new and unknown
situation.

When we call on intuition, we are assuming that
somewhere inside us, we know. Somewhere inside us, we
understand. Somewhere inside us, we can find the
handle, a way of approaching the unknown that we wish
to explore. When we "reach out" with our heart to probe
the unknown, at a very subtle level of feeling, of experiencing, of knowing, we are drawing on an inner wisdom.
Past experience comes up to provide us with a helpful
basis for comparison. But it is very subtle, like reaching

into a pocket or purse that's chock full of forgotten stuff and asking, "What is it that I'm feeling? What am I sensing? How can I know and understand what it is? How am I responding to this situation? The response is there, but how can I perceive it?" The heart's way is to use imagination to help us in that perception.

Imagination and memory are very much connected. Both draw upon patterns deep in the mind. The Intuitive Heart then uses the imagination to create, through our memories, a model or map to guide us through an experience. In much the same way, a poet goes into the intangible realm of subtle feelings and connections, of subtle patterns perceived, and finds just the right words to bring up just the right images that help us connect with feelings that otherwise might have passed us unnoticed.

You do this, too. We all naturally use our imagination to help us picture our subtle feelings so we can understand what they are telling us. Often we don't notice that we are using our imagination because we take it for granted and because what we imagine seems so real.

Beginning in childhood, for example, we imagine monsters and boogeymen that mirror our often-frightening inner feelings about life. All of us, nightly, have dreams that employ the imagination to picture our feelings in the language of stories. In our relationships, we are masters at detecting and decoding subtle information. A woman, for example, may feel that something is not quite the same with her husband, that he isn't interacting with her in his usual manner, and she may imagine that he is "distant." Here, her imagination creates a metaphor to help her explain to herself what she is feeling. In economic business, investors imagine a "bear" or "bull" type of energy behind the scenes, influencing buying and selling patterns on the stock market. You can come up with your own examples of how the imagination is used to give subtle feelings about what is going on in the environment, a language in which to express your intuitions.

In the Intuitive Heart discovery process, you are learning how to use your imagination in an intentional manner to help you understand the unknown. As you create a teaching story from the memory that comes to you, making metaphors and forming connections, you are using your imagination in the service of intuition. Later, as you apply the insights to the unknown situation you are exploring, you will start to discover a surprising pattern of ability. *Intuition is the ability to perceive the patterns that connect.* Experiencing these connections can be wonderful, exciting, and surprising.

Discovering the Intuitive Connection: Magic or Mystery?

"So the heart be right, it is no matter which way the head lies."
Sir Walter Raleigh

Here is one of the ways I demonstrate the validity of the teaching stories we create from our memories. It's a little game that goes to the heart of what it means to make an intuitive connection.

I ask a person to play the Memory Bowl Game and allow a memory to come into his or her awareness when I clap my hands. Without the person's knowledge, I form a secret intention as I swirl my arms in circles. My intention is that we'll take the person's memory story and its wisdom and apply them to the question, "How can you improve your trust in intuition?" The results are usually surprisingly instructive.

In one case, for example, I played this game with a

man named Harry. He said his memory was of going out into the ocean and seeing his brother waving for help, as if he were drowning. The man dove in and rescued his brother. When I asked the man what that memory meant to him, he said he saw that help was needed and dove right in and helped his brother without hesitating. When the need was evident, the response was immediate.

After Harry shared these insights with me, I revealed to Harry my secret question. I asked him to see what connection he could make between my question and his teaching story.

"Well," Harry responded right away, "you should just go for it, just dive right in, follow your feeling." Good answer, and quite right! When he followed his feeling, Harry explained, the outcome was good. And that makes sense, doesn't it? Harry also said that it is easier to go with intuition when the need is strong and immediate, so one reacts quickly. Another good point.

So you can see that, while Harry's literal memory involved saving someone's life, as he drew his own lesson from the memory story, the wisdom that it contained also was quite pertinent to the silent question I had asked.

I like to play this game with a large audience, so we can compare the different answers to the same silent question. I'll ask the members of the audience to allow a memory to come to mind when I clap my hands. Then I'll ask them to reflect upon the memory to create a teaching story that contains a lesson for themselves. Afterwards, when I reveal the existence of the secret question, people are excited to see how their insights connect and fit the question.

A woman in one audience, for example, remembered a take-home exam in school. She wrote her answer, but didn't think it was very good, so she borrowed someone else's paper and copied the answer from it. As it turned out, the borrowed answer was wrong, while her original answer had been right. The lesson, she said, was an obvious statement about intuition: that we often tend not to trust what comes from within ourselves, but instead look outside, only to find that the external answer is wrong, while our internal answer is very right.

In that same audience, a man spoke up and told us about his memory of being at a pub and throwing darts. He said it was the first time he had played, and when he threw the darts slowly and carefully, they hit the dartboard but then fell out. When he threw them faster, he couldn't take as much care with his aim, but at least the darts stayed in the board. As he threw more darts, he learned that he could stop thinking so much about what he was doing and that he got better all the way around. The application to trusting intuition was obvious. When you're tentative and trying to think it through, he said, it may seem that you're guiding the situation carefully, but in fact the darts are duds. But when you just go with it, stop thinking so much about what you're doing, the darts go in and you find yourself doing better.

Another person volunteered that her memory was of learning to ride a bicycle and how wobbly it was until someone gave her a push. As she went faster, she didn't have time to think about what she was doing. What she found was that it was much easier to balance when she had some speed. This woman, too, felt her memory and its lesson were a good parable about trusting intuition.

I have found this demonstration to be a very effective training tool. The beauty of this demonstration is that it keeps participants from thinking about the question, from second-guessing what comes to them, because they don't even know that a question has been asked, much less what the question is. The best part is that it builds confidence in what we find within ourselves. It helps us discover that, in innocence, our answers have validity, that even though we are working with an unknown question, what comes up for us spontaneously still fits.

I recently saw a demonstration of essentially this same method with an audience on *Oprah.* Laura Day was discussing her book, *Practical Intuition.* She told the audience she was going to ask them to answer a question without knowing what the question was. She asked them to write down whatever came to mind. Later she revealed the question, "What do I need to change in my life now in order to bring in more joy?" Audience members were excited to see how what they wrote fit for an answer to that question. Oprah commented how wonderful it is that we are so "connected," that we can know the answers to questions that are hidden from us.

This technique, applying a person's spontaneous thoughts or images to a secret, or at least hidden, question, is a standard technique among intuition trainers and researchers. In her book, *The Key to Intuition,* Susan Mehrtens describes an elaborate program of applied research using this basic approach. She calls the hidden question the "key." Some call it the "target." By keeping the key hidden from the person calling upon their intuition, that person is blocked from thinking about the question. Their response to the question is unbiased, or innocent, apparently totally uninfluenced by the question.

But is it? There's a mystery here. The "key" technique is more than some kind of magic trick that helps you evade your conscious mind. It's worth looking at this mystery, the mystery of the intuitive connection.

Is the intuitive connection something you just make up, invent, to make the process a "success?" Is it just a coincidence that what comes to mind connects with the hidden question? Is it more than coincidence? Is it synchronicity, the occurrence of apparently unrelated events that come together in surprising and meaningful pattern, as if an overall intelligence were at work? A third alternative is that it's possible the person somehow psychically tunes into the question and obtains some telepathic information about the question that, perhaps subliminally, influences what comes to mind. If so, then the answers are not totally innocent or unbiased, but are being determined, or at least influenced, by psychic knowledge of the question. Which of these three alternatives is it? Is it any of them?

This mystery is difficult to unravel. It is the existence of this mystery that makes the Intuitive Heart discovery process that you are learning here so special. The process helps you discover your own intuition about the mystery, or to intuitively move through the mystery into a deeper appreciation for how your inner wisdom connects you with helpful paths through life's challenges.

Match Wisdom with the Experts

"Judge not by the eye but by the heart."   Cheyenne Proverb

There is a simple exercise you can practice that will help you explore the mystery of the intuitive connection. It will build your confidence in this intermediate phase of learning the Intuitive Heart discovery process. It also will build your confidence in your intuition, confidence that you can use later to find answers for yourself, when you do know what the questions are.

Select a book that you have enjoyed, that has inspired you in some way. Perhaps you will choose the Bible, the *I Ching,* or some self-help book. Whatever it is you select,

I'm going to show you how to learn about your own intuitive understanding of the passages in that book, how to explore within yourself and come up with some wisdom that connects you at a higher level to those passages.

First, you need to set an intention, just as you do when using the intuitive process to help someone else. Your intention is that you are doing this for the purpose of coming to a greater appreciation of your intuitive ability. Your intention is that you are learning to use your intuition for making connections and understanding a passage in the book. Although this is a lighthearted demonstration, don't approach it as a trick. You really do want to access a higher part of yourself that is more profoundly involved in this process. Use a book that has had an impact on your life for an easy way to get into the spirit of this exercise.

Once you have set your intention, then, without opening the book completely, put your finger or a card into a randomly selected place and tell yourself that a particular spot on either the left or right page will be your target passage. You don't know what is there yet, but your intention is to look at that spot, and that is the passage that you want to come to understand.

Still without opening the book, take yourself through the Intuitive Heart discovery process: Follow your breath. Move into its flow. Then let a memory come that you will use to make your own wisdom connection with the unknown passage in the book. Just trust the first memory that comes.

Take a moment to write that memory down or to talk it out with yourself as if you were talking to a friend. One of the things I have found in working alone is that, if you don't have someone else there as a prompter, you need to find a way to get past just sitting there and thinking about what you're going to do and then trying to do it. It's difficult in that situation to know when you're actually doing it and when you're just thinking about it. Also, when you're just thinking about it, you tend to move faster, think in shorthand, and skip past potentially revealing statements and ideas. It all happens so quickly, you may miss the intuition!

Even though it takes extra time, many people tell me they prefer writing out their memory. Usually, I talk it out to myself, unless I'm in special circumstances where that isn't a good idea. You may even want to tape record yourself if you find talking it out is helpful, so that you can listen to it again. Experiment and decide what works best for you.

When you have told or written out your memory, then go on to talk about what it means to you, what you have learned, or now can learn, from that experience or memory. When you've done that, it's time to open the book to the preselected spot and read the passage you find there. See what kind of connections you can make with the memory you got and its lessons.

At first, you'll look for obvious connections, but don't be afraid to go beyond that and "create" connections. Intuition is a matter of seeing patterns that connect, and patterns can come from a variety of places. Even if you feel you are making up a pattern in order to have a connection, that's okay. The connection that you make up might turn out to be a very surprising and valuable approach to that passage and to some issue in your life. So just practice with this process, again in a lighthearted manner, until you are comfortable with it and have discovered that it's an interesting and valuable approach.

The exercise serves many purposes. For one thing, it helps you to develop the ability to use the Intuitive Heart discovery process alone, without a partner's question. It also gives you an opportunity to reflect upon the mystery of the intuitive connection. As you explore your own private intuitive discoveries, you'll begin to appreciate whether or not your intuition provides you with original and helpful insights about passages in your favorite book. If you begin to find that you can come up with interesting intuitions, not only will your confidence begin to grow, but maybe your curiosity will begin to excite your imagination about what makes intuition work. If so, you also may begin to appreciate what is special about the Intuitive Heart discovery process.

The Wisdom of Using Memories to Evoke Intuition

"Now that my ladder's gone,
I must lie down where all the ladders start,
In the foul rag-and-bone shop of the heart."
William Butler Yeats, *The Circus Animals' Desertion*

One of the first studies of intuition in the real world appeared in the book, *Executive ESP,* by Douglas Dean. He successfully tested his own intuition that those corporate executives who were more successful also had more effective intuition. He compared the intuitive performance of CEOs whose company stock had increased during the last year with CEOs whose company stock had declined. His test for intuition was rather crude, but it proved the point. He asked the executives to guess the output of a computer that was going to generate a series of 100 random digits. It was like guessing an enormous lottery number. He found, as predicted, that the more successful CEOs scored much higher on this outrageous task than the less successful CEOs.

What's interesting for us is that when these CEOs were asked about their experience picking the numbers, they said that they didn't have a feeling of knowing what the specific results would be. They didn't have an experience of seeing into the future and realizing what numbers would come up. Instead, they experienced the task as a guessing game. They were, they said, just "making [the numbers] up."

Even though their task was much different from the kind of intuitive tasks we're taking on with the Intuitive Heart, I'm convinced that these CEOs were basically doing what you are learning to do. In a complex situation where there were many unknown factors involved, the executives were responding to something within themselves, regardless of how they experienced it—guessing, making it up, having a hunch or whatever—to answer a question about an unknown event they would learn about in the future.

In the Intuitive Heart discovery process, you are doing something essentially similar. But you are learning to do something beyond that as well. You are learning to bring together the experiences and memories that your Intuitive Heart selects into a teaching story, a metaphor that orients you, that has "heart" and personal meaning, that brings your values to it so you can respond as a caring person to the situation on which you're focused. In other words, you are going for more than "Just the facts, ma'am," and looking for guidance and understanding.

Now, I can give you another answer to the question, "Why a memory?" Why do we approach intuition through this combination of tuning in, getting a memory, making wisdom from it, and so on? Why not just have a direct vision of some sort into the answer, some kind of ESP?

The answer is that we value intuition (and approaching it through memory) because it provides us with *guidance*. It's not just a means of getting knowledge or a set of facts; it provides understanding and wisdom.

If ESP is the ability to *sense* things without use of the traditional senses, to see around "corners" of time or space, then intuition is the ability to understand the *meaning* of things. Suppose you had just ESP. What would you do with the facts that you might sense through ESP? How could you know what those facts really meant? Intuition, on the other hand, is the ability to turn within for guidance about the facts, guidance for applied understanding. Intuition is holistic. It provides guidance and wisdom, and puts the knowledge in a context, because the values of the person having the intuitive experience come into play.

One image that helps me understand the difference between ESP and intuition is the library. With ESP, I may be able to sense words and pictures from any book I hold in my hand. But intuition allows me to do something more valuable. It helps me, when I have a particular need, to walk directly over to the book and open it to the needed passage within it, the one that has just the perfect information in it to accomplish my mission, to meet my need. It helps me get the job done!

Intuition adds wisdom to ESP. And what is wisdom but what we have learned from experience?

We each have a whole treasure chest full of experiences. From our experiences, we grow and develop as people. How we come to think about those experiences, what we gain from them, becomes our body of wisdom. In facing the unknown, in facing a new situation, we do not come unarmed or empty-handed. Instead, we have a wealth of experience on which to draw for guidance. In intuition, when we confront a situation that involves unknown factors, we can draw upon our experiences for guidance in how to deal with that which confronts us at the moment.

Of course, the situations we confront are not exact

replicas of something from our past, and we're not going to do exactly the same thing we did back then. But intuition's wisdom enables us to bring a certain kind of understanding, based on past experience, to provide us with an orientation, an approach, to new situations, even though the new situations have unknown factors.

We've seen how metaphors help us understand the unfamiliar in terms of the familiar. What's incredible is how our intuition seems to "know" just what would be a perfect memory to create a teaching story that will provide the perfect metaphors for generating creative insights into the unknown. Now there's a mystery for you!

Practice Builds Confidence

"Let us not pretend to doubt in philosophy what we do not doubt in our hearts."   Charles Sanders Pierce, *Collected Poems*

Even as you may doubt your own intuitive ability, there's no doubt that practice will increase your confidence. Practice, practice, practice makes perfect. You begin to get a feel for the process. The discoveries you make cast doubts aside.

Your practice moves through stages. You practice getting memories you hadn't thought of for some time. You practice making stories out of those memories. You practice turning the stories into lessons that show you your wisdom and bring you insights. You practice generating teaching stories to apply to unknown situations and questions, such as book passages and questions posed by others. And then you practice dealing with your own challenges, questions that you know, and explorations into the unknown of your choice. All these skills will come in time as you practice each step of what you are learning.

For now, however, just play the Memory Bowl Game and let a memory pop to the surface. Tell yourself the story of that memory, using whatever method you prefer. When you've finished, explore the memory further, looking for the meaning, the message, the teaching that the memory's metaphor carries. Chances are you'll find that the metaphor and its lessons apply to some issue in your own life, even when you didn't ask a question. But the point here is simply to let you practice searching for the metaphor and its wisdom.

As you are thinking about practicing, I've been playing the memory game, too. I'm remembering a time that I bought a house that was in shabby condition on the outside. I decided to get rid of the old brick doorsteps at the back of the house and to replace them with a deck. So I got a mason's chisel and a sledgehammer, and I began to take the steps apart. My expectation was that under the outer layer of bricks, I would find more layers of bricks and that it would take me quite a while to demolish the steps. But I was in for a surprise. Once I got some of the outer bricks loosened, I saw that underneath was not much of anything. In fact, the steps were hollow and rested on a pile of broken brick pieces.

As I look at this memory, what comes to mind is that I was faced by what I thought was a very challenging task, one that would be time-consuming and difficult, that would take me away from other work I needed to do. When I made a start, however, and I broke through the surface, the problem just fell away. There wasn't nearly as much work there as I had anticipated. This tells me to just get in there, get started, just keep chipping away and see how the problem may become much less daunting than I originally thought.

It's a very appropriate lesson for the challenges I faced in writing this book, which is a synthesis of my decades of research, research that has resulted in file cabinets full of information and data. It also is a pertinent piece of wisdom to pass on to you about working with your intuition and with the Intuitive Heart method. Just get started. You'll find that it's easier than you think, and you'll see some surprising results.

8

Step Six:
Learning from Feedback—
Sharing Heart to Heart

"The realization of 'meaning' is therefore not a simple acquisition
of information or of knowledge, but rather a living experience that
touches the heart just as much as the mind."

Marie-Louise von Franz

*M*y friend, Jane, volunteered to let me practice my
intuitive storytelling skills with her. So I went through
the steps of the Intuitive Heart discovery process to retrieve a memory.

To help me focus my intuitive storytelling, Jane had
agreed to think of a question or concern she had in her
own life, and I was to speak to it with my story. I had gone

through the steps of following my breath and reaching out to her and her concern with my heart.

I remembered when, as a young boy, my parents finally allowed me to mow the lawn with the power mower. It was a gasoline-powered, self-propelled, reel-type mower, and only my parents had used it up to that point. I was very happy to be able to use it myself. I was going back and forth, up and down the yard, guiding the mower. My mom was sitting outside on the patio while I mowed. I was determined to show her that I was capable of handling the lawn mower. As I maneuvered the mower around the trees, turning it expertly and deftly, I would glance at Mom to see if she was noticing how well I was doing. Then the mower got a little out of hand, and I swerved with it and missed a strip of grass. After I regained control, I glanced up quickly towards my mother, who was absorbed in something else and hadn't noticed my little mishap. So I quickly backtracked to cut the strip of grass that I had missed.

That was the memory that flashed into my mind and its story, which I shared with Jane. The memory and story don't sound like much, do they? They didn't sound like much to me, either, but I continued.

As I searched my heart for the story's wisdom, I talked about what meaning that memory might hold for me. I said that I knew that my mother's approval had meant a lot to me when I was young. Everyone wants their mom's approval, I suppose, but my mom always seemed upset, depressed, or unhappy, so I worked extra hard to try to make her smile. As I talked, I understood that this was something that had continued as I grew into an adult and that, eventually, it had translated itself into a need for other people's approval, particularly women's. As I explored these thoughts aloud with Jane, I began to talk a little about the problems that this need for approval had caused me. For one thing, it always had made it more difficult to get centered within myself. I was good at knowing what other people wanted, but not so good at knowing what I wanted.

It wasn't easy to share these thoughts. I felt that I was exposing some of my painful secrets and some of the less dignified aspects of myself. But it was a heartfelt sharing, something I had agreed to do in order to try to help Jane with her concern. While it was clear that I had touched on something that was an issue for me, I didn't see how it could relate to Jane. When she told me the question she had on her mind, however, I was very much surprised.

Jane had wanted to know whether or not the therapist she had just begun seeing would be able to help her with her relationship with her mother. She explained that she, too, had a deep need for her mother's approval, and that it had been a major issue in her life. She said she had gone into therapy when she noticed her own daughter behaving in ways that reminded her of herself as a child, looking for Mom's approval. I listened in amazement and growing pleasure as Jane said she found my story to be right on the mark. She said she was particularly impressed with my personal insight about my mother's depression and my efforts to cheer her up, and then my feeling that I hadn't succeeded, which grew into a need to somehow perform for the world, to cheer it up, so it would recognize and love me.

As Jane and I continued to talk about the experiences that my lawn-mowing memory had opened up for us, we felt very close to each other. We realized we were very connected in some important way, sharing similar feelings. We also were very surprised at the things we had in common and how we had somehow "stumbled" onto this connection through my "little story."

Feedback Is an Important Discovery Process

"Where hearts are true, Few words will do."
                              A.B. Cheales, *Proverbial Folklore*

This simple example from my own experience illustrates well the final step in the Intuitive Heart discovery process: sharing the feedback. This final step is quite important in your training and the development of your intuitive ability. It is also full of its own rewards.

As you recall, my basic discovery of the Intuitive Heart is that it is most naturally invoked when you experience caring or compassion for someone else. Therefore, both to stimulate your intuition and to validate it, I have recommended that you practice the Intuitive Heart discovery process by offering to share it with someone else. This final step of the process, the sharing of feedback, is your major opportunity to learn how—and how well—your intuition operates. It is here that you will develop confidence in the insightful power of your Intuitive Heart. You'll need this confidence in order to trust your Intuitive Heart enough to follow it on your own into the unknown that lies before you.

But there is more to the sharing of feedback than simply learning if your intuitive story was "right" or "wrong." The sharing of feedback with another person is an adventure in itself. Not only does it involve your self-disclosure, but it involves a fair degree of intimacy between the two of you. For some people, this intimacy is an added benefit of the Intuitive Heart discovery process. For these people, the quality of intimacy that the process creates becomes one of the main reasons for practicing it. For other people, the intimacy is a serious obstacle. You'll have a chance to see in which camp you feel most closely identified. In either case, the intimacy of the feedback sharing process brings up some important issues about exercising your Intuitive Heart. Before we look at these issues, let's review briefly the steps leading up to this sharing of feedback. To practice the Intuitive Heart discovery process, you can use the approach I used with Jane. Ask people with whom you feel comfortable if they will help you practice your intuitive storytelling skills. When someone agrees, you ask that person to silently choose a personal concern, a challenging situation or dilemma, something going on in their life for which a fresh perspective could be helpful, but without telling you what it is. You then get into the intuitive state of flow by following your breath. Appreciating your breathing as a gift enables you to focus feelings of gratitude in your heart, thus elevating your consciousness. Next, direct the love blossoming in your heart toward your partner, making the heart connection. You give yourself permission to care about your partner, and you take that person into your heart. You give yourself permission to share of yourself if it will help with your partner's concern, and you invite a personal memory to appear that will prove helpful. You accept the first memory that comes to you and describe it aloud to your partner, weaving it into a story about the situation and what happened. As you speak extemporaneously, you search your heart for wisdom and, speaking from the heart, reflect upon and explore the story for the wisdom it contains for you personally at that moment. Then, in the final step, you ask your partner to reveal to you what the concern in question was and to give you some feedback.

It is during this feedback-and-discussion stage that the value of your story becomes known. It is also an important time for you to receive validation of your intuitive abilities. It feels risky to go out on a limb with such personal revelations. All the while you are telling your story, you won't know if it has any bearing on the person's concern, or if it might be merely amusing, or even boring. Getting feedback is important in becoming more familiar with how your intuitive ability functions and how much it can be trusted. Learning how to receive and process this feedback becomes an important step in the development of your skills in handling your intuition.

It is only natural for your partner to react to your story. The person has been listening attentively, intent upon discovering what it might have to do with them or their question. Often, they are bursting at the seams to respond and tell you the meaning your story has for them. Sometimes, however, they may be slow to react, pondering what you have said, not sure of what they think about what they have heard. Sometimes they respond more to your story, at other times to your reflections upon its wisdom. Sometimes they look at your story in very literal terms, and other times they make broad leaps, using what you've shared with them in unexpected ways. In all cases, if you will accept your partner's reaction and the situation as a learning experience for both of you, the conversation that ensues can be quite enlightening.

Let's look at a few typical situations that come up in the sharing of feedback. We'll look at how to respond to them in such a way that both you and your partner receive some value from the discussion. You also will receive deeper insights into the workings of your Intuitive Heart and its desire to reveal a loving perspective on life.

Getting Past the Mind-Reading Mentality

"Enough of Science and of Art;
Close up those barren leaves;
Come forth, and bring with you a heart
That watches and receives."

William Wordsworth, *The Tables Turned*

For many of us, intuition means the ability to see around corners. The ESP, or psychic, aspect of intuition may be what many of us find most exciting. It is natural to want to "test" ESP when exploring the Intuitive Heart discovery process. After all, isn't it supposed to give you access to information not otherwise available? It is, indeed, but your Intuitive Heart is ultimately directed toward providing you with *guidance*. To give you guidance involves putting information into a context that helps you to understand its meaning and significance for you. It also means looking at possibilities and strategies for navigating through life situations. Facts are just facts. How they are used separates the fools from the wise.

It's natural, especially when you are just learning, to want to turn the Intuitive Heart discovery process into a mind-reading game. There is the suspense of the secret question. When the question is revealed, people automatically look for connections. There is often a tendency, on the part of both the intuitive storyteller and the partner who has provided the secret focus, to get caught up in the surfaces of the memory, responding to the literal connections between the two. That's okay, but don't let the discovery process stop there. Don't forget that the goal is to move into the higher, more meaningful wisdom that the memory carries from the heart. It's okay to look for the proof of ESP, but don't let that blind you to the more significant dimension of guidance. The heart wants to go deeper.

I remember Bill, for example:

Bill came up with a memory about his brother's
death. He had taken some of his brother's things for
himself. At first, he felt guilty about it, but as he grew
older, he realized that those things were symbols for
aspects of his brother's personality that he had
taken into his own, traits he had valued in his
brother and thought were missing in himself. As
they gradually became parts of him, Bill began to
think of these as his brother's legacy.

Bill had been sharing with Linda, who responded
very enthusiastically to Bill's memory. She explained that she still was grieving from her mother's
death two years before. She was really touched that
Bill had connected with the feeling of grief over the
death of a loved one. She and Bill both were very
excited at the synchronicity of Bill's story involving
a death in the family and made a point of telling me
all about it. I was pleased at the connection they
had found, but I suspected that they were so focused on the synchronicity that the real sharing
hadn't gotten started.

With a little coaching, however, I got them to take
the feedback process further, to talk about what the
memory meant to each of them. When I asked Bill
what connections he could see, he went into greater
detail about his difficulty in accepting his brother's
death, the great comfort he eventually took from
the things he had kept, and the ways he found his
brother in himself.

As she listened to the meanings and lessons Bill
drew out of his memory story, Linda soon saw that
there was more than just grief in common in their
experiences. She told us about how her mother al-

ways had been her biggest booster, had really believed in her, and that, for some reason, Linda always had had trouble accepting her mother's image of her. Linda said she still cried when she read a letter her mother had written her just before her death, in which her mother had talked about her belief that Linda would do well in life, that she had what it takes to succeed.

As they continued to talk and share and look into their hearts, Linda and Bill saw that she was in the same place Bill had been as a boy. Her mother's letter represented a "lost" piece of herself, something that she felt she was missing, and she held on to the letter as a representation of that lost piece. But unlike Bill, she had not yet taken the next step of finding the things her mother had spoken of within herself and finding peace with them. She said Bill's story was a real wakeup call for her about the inner work she needed to do in order to get on with her life and to become whole.

Had they remained stuck in their surprise at the synchronistic "hit" of Bill's memory, as people commonly do when they are first learning the Intuitive Heart discovery process, they would not have gotten to the real connections they shared, to the vitally important message of wisdom that Bill's heart had chosen in order to help Linda.

There is no question that these synchronistic connections are exciting, especially at first. They often are very surprising. People talk about how they get goosebumps, about their hair standing on end, when the other person's memory is so similar to their own concern. Sometimes, even this level of connection is a very emotional experience, bringing tears. The connections that happen can be very powerful.

But it's important that you learn to keep your eye on the intuitive "ball." The real game isn't to use intuition to read someone else's mind. That's a small game, although it helps develop some confidence. The real game is to be helpful, to find a path of harmony through a situation, to an outcome that is loving and constructive to one's development.

It's a little paradox, but your heart can resolve it. You work with others to develop your confidence in your intuition. To invoke your intuition, you work in a situation where you can be helpful. If you are sincere in wanting to be helpful, then you can't always get "proof" that you were intuitive. Sometimes you are helpful in other ways. There is no predicting how people will make connections with your story. Sometimes it makes you wonder what is going on, as this next story made me wonder.

Accept the Unexpected

"The heart of man is made to reconcile contradiction."

David Hume

Dora was one of my partners early in my exploration of the Intuitive Heart discovery process. Her reaction to my story taught me an important lesson.

When I made a heart connection with Dora, I immediately saw myself standing in front of a teacher's desk. It was from fourth or fifth grade. I'm not sure which, but in my memory, I could see myself going up to the teacher's desk. On the wall behind it hung the "hall pass." It was a large wooden sign that you carried with you when you left class to go down the hall to the restroom. It was your permission to be in the hall instead of in class. As I recalled reaching for the hall pass, I realized that I was concerned about the girls in the classroom. I was a bit annoyed that they would know that I was going to the restroom. I don't know why I was thinking about such things, but I was clearly embarrassed about the girls thinking of me at the toilet in the restroom.

I reluctantly shared this memory with Dora, embarrassed once again by the topic. I bravely went ahead and, closing my eyes, began to reflect upon the memory, searching my heart for wisdom. Now I don't recall very much of the wisdom I discovered and shared with her, but it had something to do with the difference between the sexes, both the body curiosity and the body shyness between males and females and how it seemingly never ends. I remember talking for a long time, because as touchy a subject as it was for me, somehow, I was even less enthusiastic about having to face Dora's reaction.

When I finally did stop talking and opened my eyes, I saw that Dora was crying. She startled me by exclaiming with apparently powerful relief, "It's the kitty litter!" She gave me a big hug and added, "Now I won't have to send Miss Buttons back to the pound!"

I had no idea what she was talking about. I sat there patiently for a few moments while Dora became more composed. She then calmly began to explain to me her situation and the question she had held in her mind. Dora had recently introduced a new kitten into her home. Trouble was brewing, however, because Miss Buttons wasn't using the kitty litter. Instead, she was using the carpet. Dora didn't understand why and was hoping my intuitive storytelling skills would help her figure out the problem. It had indeed! She had another cat, Mr. Tim, a neutered male, who had been with her for several years. The problem was that she was assuming that Miss Buttons would have no objection to sharing the kitty litter box with Mr. Tim. Apparently, Ms. Buttons had some modesty concerns similar to my own!

I not only was surprised by how Dora had used my story, but also relieved as well. Later, I had a chance to puzzle over my memory, amazed at coming up with such a recollection. The theme of my story, and its philosophical overtones concerning the tension between the sexes, was quite different from Dora's concern, and yet it did relate, in an odd way.

I also pondered the fact that, during the telling of the tale, I was feeling quite uncomfortable. It seemed unnatural to feel that queasy, but that was the way I was feeling. I wondered if this was the way Miss Buttons was feeling. It appeared to me to be a classic example of intuition at work, where the person was being guided, but not even suspecting it.

Was it intuition? I do know that Dora was helped by my story. She got the information she needed. Did I get validation? In a strange way, yes. What I thought was a silly memory proved to have great value. Sometimes we reject our intuition because we think that the thoughts which come to us are meaningless. Dora proved me wrong.

Going to the Heart of the Matter

My heart suspects more than mine eye can see.

William Shakespeare, *Titus Andronicus*

Another thing that I see regularly is how intuition can answer the real question, how it can arrow right past the questioner's reluctance, answering the genuine question when a superficial question was asked instead.

Often the people you approach to help you with your intuitive storytelling skills won't realize at first the profound experiences the Intuitive Heart can bring, or they may not wish to really open themselves up to the exercise. So, they may ask a question that seems to have little importance or that is about someone else, such as a friend or spouse. Don't worry about it. Things usually work out if you'll accept their question while continuing to explore with them for a little deeper answer. Sometimes you'll find out why, of all the innocent questions they could have asked, they asked the one they did. You don't have to be a psychoanalyst to get to the heart of things, but you do need to be open-hearted in your own sharing. Let me tell you about a time that shows you how the wisdom of the Intuitive Heart can reach past surfaces to touch on what is important:

Once, when I was practicing my own Intuitive Heart skills, I asked an acquaintance named Karen if I could practice them with her.

The memory that I shared with her was about when I first met a woman I was to marry. My first image of this woman was of her painting and of her expressions as she painted. I told Karen a lot about how I valued this woman's artistic talent, which attracted me to her. I also told Karen how, with the woman's encouragement, I came to discover a similar artistic talent in myself. This talent led me to do quite a bit of painting of my own. I told Karen that now I could see how I had placed in my wife a lot of my own feelings and values about artistic expression that I wasn't owning for myself and how, over the years, I learned that I needed to express myself. I also realized that often I see a native value of my own only after first encountering it in someone else, and that I tend to spend a lot of time fussing over the other person's ability when I should be recognizing this talent or issue in myself.

When Karen told me her question, I realized that she had kept me somewhat at a distance by asking a question about her husband instead of herself. She wanted to know whether he should leave his current job and get a better job that would make him happier. But her next comments surprised me. She explained that, even though she had asked about her husband, in listening to my memory, it had brought up a lot of things for her that made her aware of ignoring her involvement with her own abilities.

"I've really been focused on my husband's career all these years," Karen explained, "and I looked at my own as sort of filling in financially. And now I realize, after listening to you, that I should have asked you a very different question that really is more about me and some problems that I have with self-confidence and self-expression, which are very big issues for me."

At first Karen had viewed my efforts as something akin to an act of entertainment. She really didn't think she had a significant question to ask me; she was just indulging me because we were friends. As I told my story, it didn't appear to me to address her question. Yet, once I heard her reaction, I realized that the memory I got zeroed right in on the major concern about herself that really was operating behind her superficial question about her husband's job. She had been in denial for years about that issue, hadn't wanted to address it. But she left our conversation with a life-changing insight, happy with her unexpected understanding of her real problem and some guidance toward solving it. She went away visibly affected by what happened. She learned something by reflecting on the fact that she chose to ask a question about her husband rather than for herself. She made an important discovery about herself—a discovery that my Intuitive Heart had addressed even though she hadn't asked that question. It was a major affirmation for me, and helped me to really trust the process I was developing.

You may have this kind of experience as well. The important thing to remember is that, when other people are giving you their feedback, just be curious and open. Their sharing probably will evoke more thought and sharing on your part. This back-and-forth conversation often can lead to the real issues in their lives, even when their questions seem superficial.

It is these types of encounters, in fact, that often stay in my mind for a long time as I try to understand what they mean. I have developed a real appreciation over the years for the Intuitive Heart's wisdom, for its ability to be in the right place at the right time, to be in the right way with the right memory at the right moment for that person. It's a mystery how we can, without knowing how, offer just what the other person needs to hear. It's a mystery that, when we search our hearts for wisdom, when we go into our hearts for knowledge, we can, without knowing exactly how, bring forth what is needed, both for ourselves and the other person. It's a mystery that is fun to explore with your Intuitive Heart.

Discover All That Your Intuitive Heart Knows!

"Search thine own heart. What paineth thee
In others in thyself may be."

John Greenleaf Whittier

It was my experience with Peter that helped teach me to go below the story's surface, to mine it for the important lessons that the Intuitive Heart knows are there:

The memory that came to me involved climbing a mountain. It was not a big mountain, certainly, but it was a mountain to me, and a physical challenge as well. I kept stopping and looking to see how far I still had to go, and I was tired and discouraged and wondering if I would make it. Finally, I just had to bear down and keep looking only at the trail right in front of me and chanting a little song to myself. Eventually, in that way, I reached the top.

When I searched my heart for wisdom, "Whistle while you work!" was a phrase that came to mind. I discussed the value of staying focused on the present moment. I always tend to look ahead to the completion of a task, and I discourage myself when it isn't getting done as fast as I think it should. Of course, if I can stay centered on simply doing the task, the finishing will take care of itself, and I enjoy myself more in the meantime.

As it turned out, Peter was asking about a situation at work. He was facing a block in achieving a goal and didn't know if he ever would succeed at it. He was trying to establish a new program and was running into a lot of opposition. He had been wondering if he should abandon the effort. He wanted to know what, exactly, was the problem with his project. It wasn't difficult for him to look at my memory story and to interpret the top of my mountain as his work goal. He quickly gleaned the lesson that instead of trying to see far ahead into the future, he should just keep his nose to the grindstone and that, ultimately, it would work out. He could see that he was just frustrating himself by constantly comparing where he wanted to be to where he was, by always dwelling on how much further he had to go and how little progress he had made.

Peter and I both found a pretty good lesson in that story. It was one we both needed to hear. Fortunately, we didn't stop there.

I was able to tell Peter that, in the process of climbing my mountain, I learned something important about just enjoying the climbing, about not being so focused on getting to the top but on finding the pleasure in just putting one foot in front of the other. Also, I saw that when I focused so intently on getting to the top, I neglected to pay any attention to my companion hikers. As I allowed myself to enjoy the climbing process, my attention widened, and I tossed a few friendly comments at the other people who were making their way to the top along with me. I enjoyed the banter, and the climb became progressively more fun and easier.

As I talked about this experience, I told Peter that it also reminded me of a couple of times in my life when I was an employee in a company and became aware of how much talking and politicking were required to get anything of real value done, of how long all that can take compared to how quickly things move once everyone buys in to the project. I reflected on how I had to adopt the attitude of going slowly and just enjoying the interaction with the other employees, using it as an opportunity to bond with them as I went through the sometimes very slow process of getting a new program into place.

In response to my sharing, Peter began telling me more about his project at work. Part of the problem was other people who did not necessarily favor what he was doing. He realized that he saw these people as obstacles. He learned from my sharing that he needed to treat these people as colleagues. He should risk having the project scuttled by accepting their viewpoints and taking more time to talk things over with them.

Peter and I discovered that we both had a tendency to look to the goal and overlook the importance of other people in reaching our goals. Relations at work are important work skills. When you need other people to help you get a job done, you can't just force it, as much as you would like to. Peter and I both needed to be reminded of that important fact.

Because we didn't stop at the surface level of sharing the connection between his question and my story, Peter and I ended up having a very interesting conversation about work and the personal growth that it could offer us if we were open to an attitude adjustment. We helped each other reinforce some important learning about working with other people. Peter left our sharing with some real insights into himself and others, into the process of building a consensus and into the pleasure of the process itself, not just the goal. I gained the same benefit, as well as discovering just how insightful my Intuitive Heart could be.

Getting Past the "Just Coincidence" Barrier

"The Heart knows, the Thought denies. Is there no other way?"
Stephen Sondheim

You may be asking at this point, however, whether we can't see connections in just about anything? The answer is yes, but that's okay, too.

Maybe the question behind that question is, "Isn't it possible that my partner or I see connections between the story and my partner's concern that are not really there?" The answer is that if you *see* the connection, then the connection *is* there. Really.

It may help to understand this concern, about whether or not intuition sees into things, if we look at a more important question, the one by which we should judge the Intuitive Heart discovery process. That question is, "Do the insights that you are getting actually prove helpful to you or to the someone you're trying to help?" Working with this question reveals assumptions and prejudgments we have made about how the world works and that can get in the way of really understanding the working of intuition and of learning to work with it.

Any situation has multiple possibilities. What intuition is very good at is in sniffing out a possibility that will work for you. Intuition can find that one approach that can open up and help resolve a situation.

The Intuitive Heart is less interested in the question, "Will the stock market go up or down next week?" Not that intuition can't help answer that question. There are many tricks available to help you harness your intuition to answer such a yes-or-no answer. But the Intuitive Heart is more interested in answering the question, "How can I create and develop an investment strategy that leads to the greatest sense of well-being for me and those around me?" This type of question is not a simple yes-or-no type of question, but it deserves an answer, and the answer to this question will put the former question into the proper perspective.

If you think about it, in most of the really important areas of our lives, there is no such thing as one clearcut reality. Which isn't to say that intuition can't be helpful in situations of more fixed reality. A hunch not to take the usual route home, only to find later that a traffic accident had happened there is a good example. But in many of our decisions and problems, there are several ways that might be workable, depending on our values and all the other factors and people involved. It is here where the Intuitive Heart has so much to contribute.

Recall my sharing with you the story of the psychics I interviewed, whose responses helped inspire me to develop the Intuitive Heart discovery process. Each psychic gave a different answer to my question, yet each answer had its own validity. Each answer was correct in some way, even though each psychic was looking at the question through a very personalized lens. The same thing was apparent in my work with the dream circles. Each dreamer approached the unknown question from within their own point of view, presenting a story that often didn't match the particulars of the questioner's situation, but one that revealed the dreamer's point of view. They contributed from their personal approach, sharing the wisdom they had learned from their own experiences.

To say that "the fact that we can find connections between almost any two things means those connections are not real" assumes that there is only one particular connection that should be made, that there is only one possible reality to be discovered. Instead, reality is a very complex knot. Our telling of wisdom stories, whether in a dream circle or in practicing the steps of the Intuitive Heart method, is much like pulling at a knot, turning it over in our hands, to find some way into it. What we find is the storyteller's way into the situation. Stories from the heart have a way of leading us to paydirt!

The criticism that all this is just the illusion of connections misses the point. The real proof of the pudding is not in that initial "Ah ha" moment of finding some similarity. The real proof comes in the testing of the idea to see if it works in the context of the question, to see where it takes you. You can make up connections, only to find that, when you try them out, they have no practical value to the questioner or relevancy to the question. You can come up with insightful connections, but if the person concerned doesn't try them out, we'll never be sure if the insights would have worked. There are those occasions where the insights create such a strong "Ah ha" reaction, such a physical sensation of release, of rightness, that the person concerned just knows that the insight is correct. Sometimes there is a healing of attitude right on the spot. But we can't count on those special times to be our standard by which we measure the insights coming from the Intuitive Heart discovery process. We can't use that standard for any intuitive methodology.

Many inventors understand how intuition works. Their initial insight may not be a direct answer in itself, but it often leads to learning that leads to its fruition in some new development or product. Sometimes, the best way to a goal is a roundabout way because you needed to learn certain things along the way in order to get there at all. The best test of an intuitive insight is to try it out and see what results.

To evaluate the reality and value of intuition, you have to keep your eye on the goal: helping the other person. As you work with your Intuitive Heart, you will grow in confidence that you can use intuition to be helpful. It's perfectly natural to want to see the goal as "Can I perform?" because you are still learning to trust your intuition. But don't let yourself lose sight of the real point of all this: Can I help? That's why it's important that you not get lost in that initial "Ah ha" when confronted with obvious connections that elicit an emotional response. Be willing to expand the discussion, to share your experiences, to share the lessons and insights that your memory brings. It will show you the much more profound level at which we are connected, a level where our hearts can give us the wisdom to help others and ourselves.

The Intuitive Heart Creates Intimacy with the World

"There is no feeling in a human heart which exists in that heart alone—which is not, in some form or degree, in every heart."
George MacDonald, *Unspoken Sermons*

Have you ever asked someone about a relationship they were having with someone else, only to have them say, "Oh, no, nothing is going on. We're just friends."? If so, you've probably wondered if they might have been trying to deny the closeness that was developing between them and their "friend." In a similar way, when someone says that these Intuitive Heart connections are "just coincidence," that person may be trying to put some distance into the situation.

To say the connections are just coincidence keeps our relationship to the experience on a more superficial level. The skepticism focuses on the philosophical aspects of the process and on the method of evaluating ESP. Skepticism can be good, but only when it is not used as a defense against experience. Rather, it should be used as a way to keep us open to experience, not to close down our experience prematurely by a rush to judgment. Experiencing connections creates an atmosphere of intimacy. The shared experience creates "closeness." The world opening up its truths to the Intuitive Heart invites greater intimacy with reality. The Intuitive Heart discovery process is an intimate way of knowing. That intimacy brings its challenges and its rewards.

One of the things many people come to value about the intuitive process is not so much the fact of intuition itself as the intimacy of sharing that can come with it. They find that they take away from the process a new understanding of their ability to help others and of the natural healing power of intimacy.

When I ask at workshops for a show of hands of how many people discovered something surprising in common with their partner, many of the hands in the room go up. When I ask how many think they would have found this out during the typical coffee-break conversation, very few raise their hands. And when I ask how many now feel closer to their partner, the hands go back up.

It's also very telling for me to watch as I lose the attention of the people in the workshop over the course of their practice with their Intuitive Hearts. And it happens every single time. At first, it's easy to have all their attention as I guide them through the information and the steps. But as they practice, it becomes more and more difficult to get them to stop talking to their partners and to come back to the larger group discussion. They are so caught up in the wonder of what they are experiencing, and in the sharing and learning that develop at a one-on-one level, that they don't want to stop. Many of them say they also find themselves involved in telling stories they have never told before, stories that lead to catharsis and healing.

Another thing that often surprises me when we consider the intimacy of this process is how frequently the unknown question not only has some direct parallel to the memory that the partner gets but also how significant some of these questions can be, even among strangers. It's almost as if the two people have come together at some unspoken level to work as emotional archaeologists who are probing and bringing up stuff that needs to be cleared, that needs to see the light of day. When I ask how many of the questions involve things the questioners have discussed previously with other people, I don't see many hands raised. When I ask how many asked a question they haven't really discussed with anyone, hands go up all over the room. These people tell me that, because they believed their partner was entering the process with a commitment to share of themselves, the questioners felt they could ask and discuss a question that was very important to them.

Intimacy is also a challenge, more for some people than for others. Many of us are not comfortable with this kind of intense emotional intimacy, particularly in a situation with people we really don't know. You may see this discomfort expressed in the questions some people ask. If they are reluctant to "expose" themselves, they may ask a question about someone else or about an issue that apparently is of no real importance. In the role of the intuitive, you also may be reluctant to talk about some of the memories that present themselves. Sometimes, they can be embarrassing memories, that highlight what you consider to be your weaknesses or that could make you a target of ridicule or rejection. Talking about the connections in a philosophical manner, as in "just coincidence," also is, of course, another way to regulate the intimacy in the encounter.

Intimacy is a very real concern for a lot of people, and in no way do I want to minimize the importance of this concern. But again, it's interesting to watch what happens in the Intuitive Heart discovery process when I see these obstacles appearing. Intuition isn't going to find its way through or around those obstacles in every instance, and you shouldn't be disappointed when it can't. Most of the time, however, I find that the Intuitive Heart does find a way to open us up to its workings, in spite of our best efforts to remain closed off.

I certainly have some pretty embarrassing memories of my own. Who doesn't? I can be just as reluctant as the next person to share with a stranger when one of those memories comes up at a workshop. But I find in myself, and I see it in others in the groups, that going through the steps of the Intuitive Heart process, particularly the heart connection step, impresses me on a deep level with my agreement to help the other person. Even in my embarrassment, I find that my commitment and my desire to help someone else prompt me to discuss my memory anyway. Here is where helping another becomes an aid to our own unfoldment and self-discovery. Healing for the other also becomes healing for ourselves.

I initially proposed that the Intuitive Heart discovery process uses the act of caring to evoke intuition so that you can learn to trust it. So many people have found that using the Intuitive Heart discovery process is itself such an act of caring and healing that they see it primarily as a communication and relationship tool. To discuss this topic fully will have to await another book. I would predict, however, that the Intuitive Heart discovery process will make a significant contribution to the growing focus on healing heart disease through teaching intimacy skills. In his book, *Heart Illness and Intimacy: How Caring Relationships Aid Recovery,* Dr. Wayne M. Sotile discusses how the ability to share one's feelings, to talk in a self-disclosing manner that creates intimacy and connection with another person, is very healing to the stressed-out heart. Intuition hints at a special connection we have with the world, an intimate connection, and allowing our hearts to seek that natural connection is very healing.

The Intuitive Heart Encourages Us to Reach Out and Touch the World Differently

"The heart of the wise, like a mirror, should reflect all objects, without being sullied by any."   Confucius, *Analects*

Getting feedback about the stories that come from your Intuitive Heart will convince you, as it has convinced the thousands of others to whom I have taught this discovery process, that there is something going on here, something extraordinary, especially in the wonders that can result from something so natural. I know you will agree as you practice it with friends and acquaintances. You will see it even more clearly when you begin asking your intuition for guidance about your own questions.

Intuition comes out of a basic reality, one that has been little recognized or accepted in our cultural and world view, but one that people finally are beginning to talk about more and more as an underlying unity. We adopt the posture of this unity when we make a heart connection and draw another person into our heart to see what comes up. The fruits of this can be seen in the resulting feelings of oneness, bondedness, and intimacy with that person and their concerns. When you begin working with your own questions and issues, I think you also will see that this process moves you into a similar state of bonding with the things you want to understand for yourself. It is a state of knowing from the inside—

from inside yourself and from inside the concern with which you are working—and there begins to develop an intimacy with all of life.

The feedback of the Intuitive Heart method enables you to go the rest of the way in drawing close to something and understanding it from the inside. That also means understanding what we have in common with it, and learning, growing, and developing those aspects of ourselves that are like it or have an enhanced relationship to it. For example, if we are trying to understand something hurtful or destructive, we can have more compassion for those things as they operate within ourselves and others.

This final feedback step in the Intuitive Heart discovery process takes you beyond the superficial question of whether you got the "right" answer, to the point of joining with what you wish to understand and, as a result, to the point of feeling closer to it and learning from it. This bond, this intimacy with what you want to understand is significant. The Intuitive Heart's value is not just in getting a problem solved but also in coming, through this process, to feel closer and more in harmony with that which surrounds you. If you're using it to make some decision about work or a relationship or how to care for your lawn, favorite plant, or pet, of course you will be pleased and happy to get some guidance that you can test out and that works for you. But the larger picture is that you also will be able to enhance your understanding, your relationship, your closeness with your issue.

Let me give you an example of what I mean:

An organization at which I did some work hired a new director, Samuel. Until Samuel's arrival, I had been able to do things pretty much the way I thought best, so when he was hired, I admit I was a little resentful of having someone come in who could interfere with my freedom of action. Samuel began laying out new policies, looking into our operations, and deciding to do some things differently. He wasn't out to get me, but his decisions had some negative impacts on me, so I was feeling pinched. And not liking it the least little bit.

I decided to try using the Intuitive Heart process to help me find a useful approach to take with Samuel and my work in this new environment. I went through each of the steps I have been teaching you. The only difference was that I was using the process for myself, as you will learn to do in chapter 9. My desire was to make a connection, not just with Samuel but also with my work, with those whom my work served, and with my own talents that wanted to be expressed. Just going through the steps of the Intuitive Heart discovery process with this desire in mind was instructive because it gave me a chance to calm down and step out of my frustration, to look at the whole picture. That, alone, had an impact on me in terms of broadening my perspective, in seeing that I might be missing the big picture.

The memory that came up for me was of the time a school principal caught me on the playing field at recess, playing marbles for keeps, which wasn't allowed in our school. He took away my shooter, and I never got it back. I stewed over that for years, wanting to get revenge, to show him. As I worked with that memory, I saw it as a story about someone I felt unjustly took something from me that I couldn't get back and about the burden that I had carried from it for so long. I saw that, at this organization, I was operating from a similar point of view.

Very likely, I was seeing someone who was trying to do his job as my enemy because what he was doing took away the freedom I had enjoyed. I wanted to get even, get back, to treat him as an enemy. I also learned, from thinking about the principal in my memory, that I had a long-standing need to acknowledge and stand up for my rights and a need for autonomy. I saw that I needed to find a way to have that autonomy or create it for myself, even though I live in a world where other people often are in charge. Instead, I had wanted them simply to grant me autonomy.

Let me tell you, this was not the guidance I was looking for! Basically, it was telling me that I needed a major attitude adjustment and that I had been asking my Intuitive Heart to tell me how to get my way at work. But it woke me up. I recognized that getting your way is not the Intuitive Heart's calling. Its territory is to help you be more in harmony with the universe, to be able to ride along on the intelligence of the universe in order to have things work out best for all concerned.

What my Intuitive Heart did do for me was to help me clarify my values. I was feeling that I cared more about work than Sam did because I had been there longer, that he was coming in and looking at areas that I didn't think he could understand, being a newcomer, and that some of them were areas where my toes happened to be. But it also made me look at why my toes were in these places in the first place, what it was I was trying to accomplish in this job. I had been too focused on where my toes were and their getting stepped on and not enough on whether my toes were where they should be for my own well-being.

I went back through the Intuitive Heart process again,

this time surrendering to its wisdom, whatever it might be, and asking for guidance in the spirit of what would be best for all concerned—myself, Samuel, the office, the clients.

On this second round, I got a memory of being in school when I wasn't getting along with someone and of getting into a fight. My dad was angry with me about the fighting, and I got the standard parent lecture about it. My teacher, on the other hand, had a different view. She suggested that neither my opponent nor I really liked fighting but that we just couldn't seem to stop taunting each other. She thought that perhaps we each had something the other actually respected and that we wanted in ourselves, so we were jealous of it in the other person. How about, she asked, if we had a kind of duel, but not one that was a physical fight? I didn't know what she had in mind, but I was excited by the idea of a duel. So I agreed.

My teacher had us announce in class that we were going to have a paper airplane duel to see who could create the most accurate airplane. It seemed strange, but it also was fun, so we made our paper airplanes and threw them into the air.

Afterwards, the teacher asked the class what was good about each of us and our airplanes. My classmates said that my opponent threw his plane with a smile and apparent joy, and that I made very neat airplanes. The teacher gave us each a prize, and after that we no longer taunted each other or got into fights. He didn't become my best friend, but I did begin to spend time with him. He was better at sports, and I was better at academics, and I think that eventually some of each of us rubbed off on the other.

I searched that memory for its lessons, and I decided that I would ask Samuel out to lunch to share with him my history with the job and what I had been able to accomplish there, to ask him about his own background, what he enjoyed, and what he saw as his challenges in taking on the management of a new organization. So I did. We didn't become friends, but we definitely came to a better understanding of each other. Samuel came up with some interesting suggestions about ways to do what I was doing better and then summarily removed what had been an obstacle for me, making it easier for me to make my own improvements. I became a kind of spokesperson for him with others on the staff, helping them to understand the rationale for his policies and so forth. My intuition and its memory lessons not only helped me find a way of getting my needs met, but also did it in a way that brought me into greater harmony with and understanding of Samuel, of his role and my role, and of our relationship to the whole for which we both were working.

Certainly, I might have achieved the same result of having my path cleared if I had used the negotiation technique of thinking up some sort of win-win situation. But I don't think I would have experienced the same inner growth of being able to examine and understand my own developmental style and issues, and of connecting with Samuel in a way that enabled us to understand each other. By turning to my intuition for inner guidance, I also promoted a mutual respect between us and a greater vision of the whole for myself.

This is the kind of thing I mean when I say that the Intuitive Heart is not focused on simply getting the job done but also on bringing new things into awareness, on the intelligence of love that reveals, from the inside out, the inherent harmony for which we all are striving. It encourages us to approach our questions and concerns in such a way that whatever we want to know about begins to reveal itself to us. We come to have a relationship with it. We learn that intuitive knowledge is not a stable thing like the answer in an arithmetic problem. It really is a relationship you can have with life, and as you relate to it, life responds. Knowledge—truth—becomes a growing thing. This, I think, is the ultimate blessing of the feedback process.

I think you will find that, as you work with your Intuitive Heart and learn to trust it, these intimacy issues will become less important and more comfortable for you. And I think you will see that the generosity of your own willingness to share also will make it more comfortable for those with whom you practice it.

Now that I've taken you through a close look at each of the steps of the Intuitive Heart discovery process, let's next look at how to adapt the method to search your heart for your own guidance.

9

Using Your Intuitive Heart for Yourself

"In a full heart there is room for everything, and in an empty heart there is room for nothing." Antonio Porchia, *Voces*

*A*fter attending an Intuitive Heart workshop, Sandra thought she might as well work with her personal dilemma using the intuitive methods she had learned. After all, nothing else had given her an answer.

Sandra believed she had to decide soon whether or not to end her twelve-year marriage to Wes. She had paid a heavy emotional price for a long time, and the tensions in the relationship were beginning to take a major toll on her physical health, too. She still loved Wes, and he said he didn't want to lose her, but his emotional problems seemed to be as bad as ever. Sandra thought Wes did try, but he always returned to his old patterns, patterns that often cost him jobs, that alienated many of their friends, that even made her hate him sometimes. It was a terrible decision to have to make, and she had gone back and forth in her mind for weeks without being able to decide.

Sandra went through the process, and the memory she got was of a time when her older sister, Molly, was a teenager. Molly had been arrested for shoplifting and had to go to court. Sandra's parents had stood by Molly. They had hired an attorney, because they worried about her safety if she had to go to jail. But they also grounded Molly for three months and made her work to pay back the court fines and the attorney fees, over which Molly protested long and loud. Sandra asked her mother why they were being so harsh. Was Molly right, she wanted to know, in accusing their parents of not loving Molly? Sandra's mother replied, "We are doing this *because* we love her. We love her enough to make her take responsibility for her actions and their consequences."

As the adult Sandra thought about the lessons and metaphors of that memory in light of her current situation, she realized that her husband had never learned that lesson. She realized that she had been "enabling" his immaturity by making public excuses for him because she sometimes was so embarrassed by his behavior.

"I realized," Sandra said, "that before I could answer the question of whether to leave, I had to answer the question of how my own behavior might be contributing to the problem. I had made it too easy for him to act like an irresponsible child."

So Sandra temporarily postponed a decision on the marriage. Six months later, she was glad she had. When she changed her responses to what he did, Wes began to have to take responsibility himself. He became somewhat more responsible. He stopped blaming others so often for the problems in his life. He treated Sandra better than he had in a long time. He even patched things up with a couple of their friends.

A year later, events showed Sandra an even more important reason behind the memory that her intuition had used to guide her decision. Wes died unexpectedly of a heart attack. As his heart was failing in the hospital, Sandra was there to say goodbye with love and with her new respect for him.

"My intuition gave Wes and me a wonderful gift," Sandra said. "The last year of our marriage was a much happier one. We had recaptured much of our love for each other. If I had divorced him in anger and bitterness, that's what I would have carried with me always, long past the divorce and his death."

For Sandra, there no longer was any doubt that she could use her Intuitive Heart to help herself.

Beginning Steps in Working with Ourselves

"Bow down thine ear and hear the words of the wise, and apply thine heart unto my knowledge."   Proverbs 22:17

You have been learning to use the Intuitive Heart discovery process to help others with their concerns. As you've practiced using it for others, you've been getting their feedback to validate your intuition. Chances are you have seen that the process can work, that the memories that come to you inspire wisdom applicable to the question at hand. By now, you probably are very motivated to try doing it for yourself. I'm going to show you how to adapt the method so you can do just that. You'll be surprised and pleased at the guidance that the Intuitive Heart discovery process can provide for your own questions and concerns.

First, I'll describe some basic exercises you can try in order to begin using the process alone and for yourself. Then we'll examine some of the issues involved in getting guidance for yourself, things that may be part of your experience.

We already have laid some pretty extensive groundwork for looking within your Intuitive Heart for help with your own questions. You have a good basis for confidence in your ability to be intuitive about your own questions. There are two challenges that you'll probably face, however. The first is that, in working with yourself, of course, you already know the issue or question with which you are dealing. When you know the question, there is a tendency to think about it logically rather than to be intuitive about it. That awareness can tempt you to doubt your intuition, wondering if it really is some subtle form of just thinking about the question. The second challenge is that, because you have a vested interest in the answer, you may worry that you can't be objective, that your hopes and fears may get in the way. We'll look at some things you can do to help you work around these obstacles. Finally, we'll explore some of the applications of the Intuitive Heart discovery process with which you may experiment for your own benefit.

Practice Intuition with Hidden Targets

"Ask questions from the heart and you will be answered from the heart." Omaha Proverb

The first step in working by yourself that I want to show you is simply to help you appreciate that you can do this work alone. It can be a very simple thing, something that you can approach with a light and playful attitude. You can demonstrate easily that the Intuitive Heart discovery process can work for you. If you have been working with other people, who set up the questions and gave you feedback, you now can make the transition to working with your own questions and creating your own feedback.

You begin by working with hidden targets. It is easier for you to evoke your intuition, without your thoughts getting in the way, when you don't know the question or the target toward which your intuition is being aimed. When someone else sets up the question and keeps it a secret, the target automatically is hidden from your conscious awareness. Working by yourself, you have to find a way to keep your targets hidden until you regain your confidence that your intuition does know how to connect with the target, just as you did when working with partners.

Recall the book technique, where you "matched wits with the experts" through the use of a hidden target. In chapter 7, I described a method where you marked a random passage in a favorite wisdom book without knowing what that passage actually was. Then you set your intention that your Intuitive Heart would connect with that passage. You asked for a memory to come to mind that would inspire in you the wisdom to better understand the passage in the book. This method is a very simple and fun way to get started using the Intuitive Heart method for yourself.

In the book technique, the unknown passage functioned as the "question." With the hidden question exercise, you now can move on to genuine questions, questions that have real meaning for you, and you can get real answers from your Intuitive Heart.

First, get a small note pad, or prepare a dozen or more small slips of paper, about 4 inches in size. Over a period of a couple of weeks or so, think about a few situations that have perplexed you or that continue to perplex you. As these situations or topics come into your mind, give each one of them a title or a one-sentence description and write it down on one of the pieces of paper. Fold the paper and put it into a container. Over time, you will collect in the container at least a dozen or more target questions for you to work on later.

When the time comes, you'll draw a target without knowing what's written on the paper. You can use the Intuitive Heart method to connect with that unknown situation and to come up with a memory for exploration. You might want to put your process in writing, to keep a journal of your results. After you have completed your intuitive consultation, then read what's written down on the paper. See if your intuitive consultation offers pertinent advice about the situation. Again, the best way to test the guidance you receive will be to apply it.

Here's one example from my own life:

I had collected targets for about a month before I drew one out. I shook them inside a bowl and said a silent prayer that the question that I would gain the most from answering at that time would be the question that would be chosen. I pulled a folded paper out of the bowl, but instead of opening it and reading it, I connected with it through the Intuitive Heart discovery process.

The memory that came to me was of washing the white wall tires of a car when I was a boy. I recalled the time I had a car wash "business" and washed a number of my neighbors' cars. One neighbor in particular gave me some tire care products and suggested that I give more attention to the tires. I began to reflect upon how much I learned about "taking care" from having this business. I received a lot of life lessons from that work, as well as from yard work and my paper route. At the time, I also reflected upon how work is a form of relationship between worker and customer and that my own work issues continue to teach me about relationships.

When I unfolded the piece of paper, I was really surprised to read, "Should I continue to mow the lawn myself or should I hire someone?" The connection was clear for me. I recalled the number of times someone had come to the door looking for the odd job, to clean gutters, to rake leaves, and I would invariably say that I'd do it myself. I realized that it wasn't so much that I wanted to do the work, but that I didn't really want to be involved with the people who approached me.

My Intuitive Heart exercise made me realize that I was missing out on an opportunity, and that, rather than think in terms of whether or not to be self-sufficient, I also could give back to some young person the opportunity I had when I was growing up. I approached a neighborhood teenager and proposed that he mow my lawn. It worked out well, and I found myself enjoying the interaction we had, as well as not having to mow it myself. The money never had been the issue, I realized.

Rob used a variation on this method to decide about a career move. He had approached me with the question of whether or not to stay in his current job, or leave it and go back to school, or start his own business. I suggested that he envision as many different options and paths as he could that might be possible. He was to write each option on a separate piece of paper, fold it up and put it in a bowl. After a few days, he was to pull out one piece of paper and, without reading it, make a heart connection with the option written inside.

Once a day, Rob did the Intuitive Heart process in writing for one of the pieces of paper, attaching the still-folded and unread paper to his written exercise for later examination. A couple of weeks later he was finished, and he began to open the papers and compare them with his memory meditations. He said that he was really surprised at how the insights that were in those meditations connected with the options he had considered. He said it was as if he had received an expert consultation going over all of his options.

On the basis of this process, Rob decided that the best thing for him to do was to start his own business, but to stay in his job temporarily, to begin a savings plan to build up a nest egg, to use his job for opportunities to plant seeds for his business. Today he is working successfully in manufacturing and selling a health product he designed, and in training people in its use.

Using the technique of responding to hidden questions you have devised will give you even more experience in seeing how the Intuitive Heart discovery process works for you. You will be able to discover for yourself if your intuitive memories are pertinent. Can you trust your wisdom to apply to the situation? You will be able to see how a willingness to act on a situation, as opposed to dealing with a hypothetical situation, affects the kind of intuitive wisdom you get and your ability to make connections.

The Morning Forecast Method

"Wheresoever you go, go with all your heart."   Confucius

We now can progress from hidden questions to questions that are only partially hidden but also are partially known, and to using the Intuitive Heart process in a way that provides more immediate guidance to actual, current concerns. I'll explain how to use it to prepare for yourself what I call the "morning forecast."

In the mornings, I take a few moments to relax before I start my day. I go through the breath meditation, the gratitude, and the heart-blossoming process, and then I reach out and make a heart connection with my day. I visualize my day as a path, with all sorts of things, people, and events that I will meet along the path. I don't bother trying to visualize any particular encounter, but simply the path itself. Of course, I am aware of some of the events that will occur that day, but certainly not all of them, nor how they will turn out. There also will be many surprises. I want to live my day in harmony, with a joyful, loving attitude. I know that I can get very busy, rush around, and it becomes easy to miss out on opportunities to stop and smell the roses. I can easily neglect to spend time with someone who needs me or who could give me a blessing. It is easy to have mishaps. Every day is an adventure.

So I make my Intuitive Heart connection with the day

ahead and invite a memory to come to mind that I will use to discover some wisdom for myself that day. It is so intriguing to see how the memory, and the wisdom I discover in it, plays out during the day.

On one particular morning, for example, my memory was of a summer when I was six or seven years old and being "introduced" to the world:

> I was staying with my grandmother and an aunt. My aunt got up very early each morning and took me with her to her job of picking vegetables. This was a new experience for me and very hard work. I would lug this big bag of beans to the scale, sweat pouring off me in the hot weather, and my bag would be weighed. I would be given a scrip for its weight and paid at the end of the week for the beans I had picked. It was pretty miserable, and eventually I got sick (although now I can't remember if I really was sick or if I was faking it). Although it was the middle of the work day, somehow I got taken home. Later, when I felt better and wanted to go back out, my aunt said no. She explained that the people who worked there made an agreement to stay all day and that I had broken my agreement.
>
> The image that I remember most is of standing in the field with my little bag of beans, which probably was only a quarter full, and getting a piece of paper. It wasn't like a hug or money or a popsicle that I could enjoy right away. I couldn't even turn it in for money for a whole week, and at my age, I couldn't understand why I should work so hard, be so uncomfortable, for such a distant reward.

As I thought about the lessons of that memory story, I saw that, as I had grown up, I had discovered that rewards often are distant and that, sometimes, it is to your advantage to make the doing of a thing its own reward, although at six years old, I wasn't good enough at picking beans for it to be a rewarding activity. Then I thought about the meeting I had to attend that day, when I had so many other things to do. It occurred to me that, although much of what I did in the course of a workday resulted in less than a piece of paper to show for it, the rewards came later.

Although I had been resisting the idea of spending my time in the meeting, I understood that, if I could find a way to enjoy it, I might make a better contribution, not just get through it. The meeting was as bad as I had anticipated, but during it, the image of the scrip in the bean field kept coming into my mind. It encouraged me, in this tense and barren meeting where everyone wanted to be someplace else, to loosen up, to joke a little, to lighten the emotional weight of the atmosphere in that room. It made the meeting progress in a more comfortable way. It was a small contribution, but it was an enjoyable and welcome one.

I don't know whether I was laboring in the Lord's "fields" that day, but when I compared my feelings about work as a child with what I confronted in that meeting, with my experiences at other jobs, with my experience of being self-employed, I got a new sense of gratitude about the whole area of work as a learning field. In work, we discover how to harness the innate resources we have been given and to connect them back into the world, allowing the great wheel of life to revolve more easily. It was another lesson about relaxing into the flow of things, how to draw from the love that is intuition's source.

Sometimes the morning forecast proves to have a surprisingly insightful grasp of something important happening to me.

On one morning, for example, the memory came to me of being called into the principal's office:

I was sitting in my classroom when a secretary from the office came in and handed a note to the teacher. My name was called, and I was escorted out. I recall how scared I was. I thought I was really in trouble or that something bad had happened. As it turned out, the principal wanted to know if I was interested in being a street crossing guard. I was pleased at being asked, but I did have to get up earlier in the morning, which was a consideration. I took the job for a year. What I remember most was wearing the yellow belt with the strap that went over my chest and a yellow rain slicker for wet days.

As I searched my heart for wisdom to discover in this memory, I couldn't help but think that somehow it meant something was going to happen to me that would shock or jolt me, like getting a traffic ticket. I tried to stay calm, and extract the lesson for the day. The main idea I got was that something that starts out scary doesn't necessarily end that way. "Don't get worried in advance" I told myself.

Still, all during the day, I was looking over my shoulder, expecting to be surprised by something that would startle me. I tried to remember what I had told myself: Don't worry; it will turn out okay. Relative to my expectations, it turned out to be a pretty boring day. There were no shake-ups. I thought that perhaps the morning forecast just didn't apply. I was sort of glad for the failure, actually.

That evening, however, as I was reflecting on my

work, I realized that the morning forecast has been more accurate than I had thought. In fact, it still had a very important piece of guidance to give me.

The week before, a client I worked for had asked me to do something that I didn't really believe in doing. On this particular day, she asked me if I had done it yet, and I said I had not. She had some rather stern, even threatening words for me, and I was somewhat afraid. But it didn't seem right, what she was asking. Now, at home, as I asked myself, "Am I going to stick to my principles?" I suddenly thought of the morning forecast. I had been "called to my principal" and was initially scared, but later it turned out I was being handed an honor. With my work situation, I was being called to my principles, and was scared by the possible consequences. I decided to risk following through on the implications of my morning forecast. It gave me some courage, and I relaxed.

That night I wrote a calm and gentle letter explaining to my client why I thought it was wrong to do as suggested, and came up with an alternative. About a week later she gave me some kind words and explained that she had come on so strongly because she was overly concerned about the situation. She was glad, she said, that I had "stuck by my principles," because my solution was the better idea! She said I was a trusty "guard" over what was right and had offered her better "protection" than she had initially realized.

Her choice of words rang in my ears. Sometimes intuition works in ways that we simply can't anticipate!

Through the morning forecast method, I've gained a lot of respect for the Intuitive Heart discovery process. I also have learned how the interpretation of the memory stories can go in many different directions and be validated in many different ways. I really believe that if you try this "morning forecast" meditation for yourself you will discover that there is "something more" than meets the eye that is looking out for you.

Is It Intuition or Is It Thinking?

"Our first teacher is our own heart."   Cheyenne Proverb

By this stage of the game, you are ready to begin using intuition to get guidance on questions you know in advance. You can pose questions to yourself such as:

"Shall I leave this job?"

"What would be a good gift to give to Mary?"

"How can I heal the relationship with Tom?"

"Why isn't the company plan working out as expected?"

All these are good examples of questions to which your intuition can contribute useful guidance and insights.

One challenge when invoking intuition to respond to questions about which you already have some awareness, however, is how to turn off your thinking mind to make way for intuition. Even if you relax your mind so that it is relatively quiet, how do you know that it is really intuition, an inner knowing, that is coming to you and not just what you might expect from your thoughts?

The answer to this challenge is not to try to stop thinking or to disallow your thinking. Your intellect can lay a good foundation for your intuition. As Carol Ann Liaros (the intuition training expert who often works with me in training programs) says, there can be a natural progression from intellect, then to the imagination, and finally to intuition and inspiration. So do your thinking, and then turn to intuition.

It's easier to lay your thoughts aside, by the way, if you have first given them proper attention. When someone is explaining their point of view to you, it is easier for them to stop talking and listen to your ideas if, first, you give the person a good hearing and make them feel heard. Then they can be quiet and listen to you. It's the same way with your thoughts. You can say to them, "OK, I've looked into the facts, I've heard what my thinking self says, and examined what seems to be the rational answer. Now let's see what intuition says!" With an attitude like that, you are ready to allow something new to come into your awareness.

Don't fight your thinking; let it be an ally. Many times there is intuition at work in your thoughts. As you've probably noticed at times, when you are searching your heart for wisdom and looking for the message in a memory, you find later that the thoughts that came to you while talking out your ideas about the memory contained some intuitive connections to your partner. In a similar way, you can learn to trust that, when you have set the intention to receive that kind of support, intuition will be guiding your thoughts.

How Can I Recognize Intuition?

"What stronger breastplate than a heart untainted!"
William Shakespeare, *King Henry VI*

When someone asks how to recognize intuition, they usually are asking about how to evaluate or trust the information or guidance that comes their way as a result of invoking intuition. Intuition, knowing from within, can come in many forms.

Even though the Intuitive Heart discovery process instructs you to ask for memories as the seeds of your intuition, it is not always a memory that comes in response to this request. As you practice more and more with this process, you will notice that sometimes you get other types of experiences. You already may have asked yourself about the value of memories vs. other kinds of inner promptings. I teach the Intuitive Heart discovery process using memories because we all have them stored in our minds, we all can retrieve at least one, and we all can formulate a lesson that the memory contains. The natural ease of this process can build confidence in ourselves.

As you practice and become comfortable with your intuitive abilities, as you understand better how these abilities feel to you and what those feelings mean, however, you may begin to get things other than, or in addition to, memories. You may see other kinds of images. You may get feelings, either physical or emotional, or both. You may hear things, sounds or a sort of inner voice. All of these are normal and natural parts of intuition. Some people find after a while that they get many or all of these as part of their intuitive experience. Others may experience only one. A memory may or may not come. But by that time, you will be able to relax into whatever comes for you, to accept it as the way your intuition works, and to understand what message it brings.

Here is a suggestion, given by Edgar Cayce among others, for how to learn to recognize the voice of intuition. Take an issue of concern and decide what your highest ideal is for that situation, whether it is love, harmony or something else. On the basis of that value, logically think through the pros and cons of going this way or that way, working out the best decision that you can. Finally go into a meditation and ask silently whether that decision is the best way to go. If the answer is yes, the peace of the meditation will continue. If it is not the best way, the meditation will become agitated. This is one more useful technique for learning how your intuitions feel, how to begin to tell the difference between the "yes" and "no" parts of your Intuitive Heart's answers.

We seem to be able to feel whether a decision or plan is really good or right for us. I remember meeting a young woman who worked as a security guard. We discussed using intuition in gauging people, and I asked her how she used her intuition to decide whether someone on the premises belonged there or not, whether they might represent a threat of some kind. She said that her mother had taught her that everyone has the ability inside themselves to tell right from wrong and that, because of the difference in the way those two things feel, people can use those feelings to guide themselves through most any situation. The woman said she had learned to tell the difference between her inner sense of unease or apprehension and her sense of rightness, and she relied on that knowledge in her work. With experience you, too, will come to recognize the ways that intuitive information feels to you.

There is a similar phenomenon, often used by a system called "educational kinesiology," that is founded on the interesting fact that our bodies seem to know the difference between right and wrong. Practitioners use a method called "muscle testing," in which you are asked to raise your arm parallel with the ground. The practitioner pushes down on your arm as you resist the pressure. You can tell how strong the arm is in response to the person's push. Then the practitioner will ask you to say an untruth, such as to say, "My name is George Washington." Afterwards, the practitioner will push down on your arm and you will be surprised to see that you are not as strong at resisting as before. The explanation given is that telling a lie "weakens the energy field." Whatever the correct explanation, there does seem to be this reality within the body to make a yes/no distinction between right and wrong, good and bad, healthy and unhealthy. What we are saying here is that you can use the feeling in your heart area to guide you to the truth.

As you practice with this method, you will learn important lessons about how the working of intuition feels to you. Is there a sense of relaxation? A sense of rightness about it? Is there a sense that something bothers you? Do you have a peaceful heart over it, or is your heart agitated? Everyone is capable of learning to recognize these feelings in themselves and understanding their meanings to the individual. It is part of the integrity of the heart.

Learning to Trust the Heart

"A man's first care should be to avoid the reproaches of his own heart, his next to escape the censures of the world."

English Proverb

Of course, not everyone believes that the heart is trustworthy. Are feelings to be trusted? What about objectivity?

These questions bring up the second challenge in learning to use intuition as a resource for self-guidance. "How do I know," we are really asking ourselves, "if I am getting valid guidance and not simply a reflection of my hopes or fears?"

The Memory Bowl Game relies on "being reminded" by the situation, so it is reasonable to wonder, especially when you know in advance the question toward which you are directing your intuition, whether the memory that comes into mind somehow actually is a reflection of your usual reactions to the situation. We want to be "objective," meaning that we don't want our answer to merely reflect our own subjective perspective, but to be in harmony with some larger truth.

The answer to this challenge is to consider the larger objectivity of the heart, the truth that is contained in love. Now, this is a very big subject, and it would be easy to get philosophical and refer to many writers of the past. I would prefer to have you explore this question with the aid of your intuition.

First, let me suggest that you practice this meditation: Take a real situation that concerns you and think about it. Notice the types of ideas you get about that situation. Then, get into the flow state, experience gratitude for your breath, and let love blossom in your heart. Reach out with your heart to that situation, make a heart connection with it, and view it from the perspective of love. What you will want to do, regardless of your own hopes and fears in the matter, is to try to view it through the lens of love. Don't force a goal of getting answers during this practice. Simply experience what it is like when looking at the situation from this perspective. Allow yourself to enjoy the meditation. See what new insights or perspectives you experience with regard to the situation.

Practicing this meditation may verify for you that you can indeed let go of your hopes and fears for a moment and take a fresh perspective. You can let go, at least temporarily, in order to experience the good feeling of letting the love come in. Then you can verify for yourself whether it brings a very good feeling that can counteract your concern about letting go of your own position on the matter. As you practice taking situations that trouble you and embracing them with love, just enjoying that experience, just looking at them in that frame of mind, I think you soon will recognize that you are capable of adopting a different point of view. You could call it the impersonal point of view that love brings, a point of view that cares about and respects each individual, yet is coming from a place of higher love. I think that love has its own objectivity, that the heart has its own integrity, which you can learn to trust.

There is an objective side to the heart's perspective. Recall the Institute of HeartMath's research into the effects of heart meditation that I described in an earlier chapter. The institute's staff have developed a technique similar to what we are describing here. They call it the "Freeze-Frame Technique," because it asks you to take time out when a situation is stressing you. Put the situation on pause, as in a still-frame picture. Then recall the experience of loving appreciation, and let it soothe your heart. The researchers found some important effects of using this technique. One is that, when we focus on feelings of love and gratitude, there is a harmony that begins to develop among the physical systems of the body. Both the heart and brain begin to show signs of decreasing stress and increasing harmony, even in the rhythms at which they function. The researchers also found that looking at something with love enables us to stand outside a situation, to bring objectivity to it. Love takes all sides, as it were. Love accepts and can see all points of view. The heart can reconcile contradictions. In his book, *The Freeze-Frame Technique,* author D.L. Childre describes the many situations that the institute has researched, in which this method stimulates creative problem-solving. It would seem that the heart is capable of its own wisdom. Isn't that the theme of this book?

Let me give you an example from my own experience:

I had a neighbor who regularly got upset with me

because the flowers I planted at the edge of my yard would sometimes reach out onto the public sidewalk. It was a mystery to me how she could be upset by and complain about flowers, but she even went so far as to report me to the city officials. It was not a comfortable situation, and it was complicated even more by the fact that, when she walked her dog each day, the dog often stopped in front of my house to do his business. I really didn't care if the dog pooped there, but when it was coupled with her complaints about my flowers, it was just too irritating. So I told her off.

In my intuitive practice, I decided one day to look at this situation from love, just to see what it would be like. I wasn't going into it feeling that I had to do anything about it. I was just practicing for the experience. I got into the flow of my breath and made a heart connection with my mental scene of her scowling at my flowers while her dog pooped in front of my house and of me looking out the window at it, feeling very annoyed. As I did that, I was able to see it from an emotional distance, like a movie, and as I surrounded it in love, I couldn't help but laugh at the picture I was seeing. The laughter was good: It loosened me up, broke me out of some of my stiff-necked attitude, and made room for more love to come in.

As I continued to look at it in love, the scene brightened for me, and my attention was drawn to the flowers and their beauty. I felt gratitude for their existence. Then, I saw the dog and how cute he was, how lucky we are to have animal companions, how much I've enjoyed the pets that I've had, and how much my neighbor liked hers. I could understand a little more about what the world of dogs is like, how their lines are less distinct than ours. I was seeing the dog as if he were giving the flowers a gift of fertilizer, that it was all part of a cycle.

Meanwhile, I also was laughing at these two people, both of whom were frowning. I was frowning at her; she was frowning at my flowers. I understood that we both love nature in our own way, but that we both also were caught up in very human beliefs about maintaining boundaries.

As I thought more about this memory in love, and about its lessons, I could see that, even as we try to have a relationship with nature, we also feel a need to create separation, boundaries, almost as if saying the life of the spirit (and its connection with nature) and the world of materiality are not the same. That helped me to appreciate the intentions behind both my own behavior and my neighbor's, and I thought about the many ways that, through our good intentions, consequences develop with which we then have to work. We put our arms up to protect ourselves when we're afraid, for example, but they also block out our ability to see.

So there I was, in my imagination, looking out the window with my arms up to protect myself from the "assault" of this woman and her dog. And she was up in arms because she felt my flowers were getting in the way of her free passage down the sidewalk. Both were natural reactions, and both were unfortunate. I could appreciate that both of us were having natural reactions, making choices and judgments from our respective value systems, trying to make the world an expression of what we each thought was good and right, that we had a lot in common. The major difference was that we were standing on opposite sides of a line, one seeing it as bulging out and one seeing it as caving in, and we both were right—and wrong. It all was a lesson for me in how two people can have very different perceptions of the same physical event and how that has ramifications at the level of mind and spirit, how it all fits together.

So that was my experience of looking at the situation in love, through my Intuitive Heart. It was interesting and gave me several insights. I could see that already, without even intending to, I felt more compassion for both my neighbor and myself. I had found that we had some important things in common. Those insights were important in helping me let go of much of my own frustration with the situation and anger at my neighbor. At the very least, I felt better and stopped getting so worked up over it all. Sometimes, such insights also can be stepping stones to new levels of understanding between two people.

Can I Trust Myself?

" . . . did not my heart tell the truth . . . ?"

Miguel de Cervantes, *Don Quixote*

Margaret had come to me for coaching in creative consciousness. We had done a lot of work together with her dreams, and she had proven to be very good at having dreams that helped her. She learned to get advice from her dreams on various situations. From that work, we progressed to hypnosis. I coached her in self-hypnosis, and while she was in that state of rapport with her subconscious mind, I asked her questions, which she answered. She came up with some very interesting answers for herself. Then she wanted to try doing this for other people, to make the jump from creative or inspired problem solving to introducing the extra component that might be called psychic or telepathic, in order to "read" for others. We worked on this task, and she was very good at it, surprising herself. Eventually, she developed a career doing readings for others and earned quite a reputation for her ability.

I followed Margaret's work, watching with pleasure as she grew in her abilities and developed her practice. So I was surprised by the call I got from her one day. She asked if I knew a good psychic. I laughed and asked if she was fishing for a compliment. No, she replied, she needed a reading for herself, and she didn't know if she could trust what she got for herself.

I was struck by the irony of Margaret's situation. Here was a person who, by working from within herself, had developed this wonderful capacity, first to help herself, and then to help others. But now, for some reason, she didn't trust it to function for herself. I didn't understand how that could be possible.

I know, of course, that it is a common concern. I have spoken with a large number of psychics, and they all tell me the same thing. When it comes to reading for themselves, psychics generally don't believe they can be objective, and thus they aren't able to trust their own advice. By "objective," they mean a position independent of their own standpoint.

When I ask them about love as an independent, objective standpoint, the answer I get is that they feel "blocked." Getting into a consciousness of love doesn't seem to yield any answers for themselves.

I believe that all of us should be able to trust what our intuition brings, and I knew that Edgar Cayce first discovered his abilities by doing a trance reading for his own health. He continued doing readings on himself throughout his amazing career. From the evidence of the records, he was very good at doing those readings, though not as good at taking the advice he got from them. His intuition could be trusted, but he could not be trusted to act on his intuition. I wondered if Edgar Cayce's example might have something to do with the reason most psychics have a problem with reading for themselves.

I think that the problem lies not with the idea of trusting intuition, but with the issue of not being ready to act on what we know. It is really a matter of not trusting ourselves.

When a person who is perfectly capable of helping others through intuitive consultation seeks out another person, on the grounds of objectivity, it is because they have an inner knowing that they need an extra push, an outside shove to get them moving. But I am not sure that such a shove is always in our best interest.

Coming from a completely different direction than the psychics, my personal experience included extensive work for myself. I started as a research psychologist, working with others in helping them develop their skills. My method was to begin by working to develop my own skills in those areas. I learned how to remember my dreams, and I then shared what I discovered with others. I observed what they experienced as they learned to remember their dreams, following some of the techniques I had developed. I also worked with getting guidance from dreams and with dreaming for others in the Dream Helper Ceremony that I told you about earlier. From there, I went on to work with self-hypnosis, studying with Henry Leo Bolduc, the author of *The Adventure Within: Past-Life Regression and Channeling*. I learned about going into an altered state and giving answers, discourses, speeches, pep talks to myself.

Because I gained so much experience with it, I eventually developed a sort of "shorthand" for doing it, allowing the feeling of love to get me into a place to view the situation from love, very similar to the techniques we have discussed in this book. I even wrote a book about my explorations, *Channeling Your Higher Self.*

It wasn't until after that book was published that I went back to Henry Bolduc and said that I would like to try doing it for someone else. He found a person who wanted to have a reading and got a list of questions from them. Then we tried it using the process I had developed for helping myself, to see if I could help another person with it. It seemed to go all right, and later, I received confirmation from the person that my "reading" had been helpful. The person told me that a number of the things I had said were accurate and relevant to his situation, and also that he actually had acted on some of what I had suggested and was pleased with the results. This feedback was exciting confirmation for me. Reading for another person, coupled with my continuing efforts to develop exercises for furthering the Intuitive Heart training, led me to an examination of the value I placed on doing this for others and doing it for myself.

One thing I realized was that, when you do this for someone else and get their feedback, when you can see that you've really connected with something, really tapped into something, it's a major confidence builder. When you can see that you do, in fact, have the ability to provide valid intuitive guidance for another person, when what you get is confirmed for you by someone outside yourself, it's logical to wonder whether you can do this for yourself. If the answer is no, or is sometimes no, then it is important to ask what it means that you feel unable to trust it. The answer to that has to do with the two dimensions of trust that we discussed earlier, the technique of trust and the reason for trusting.

As I mentioned earlier, in the course of my research I've gotten readings from many psychics. I have found, in the long run, that using the Intuitive Heart discovery process to work for myself is a better process for me, even when I don't like the answers it gives me. But I certainly understand the appeal of the idea of using an outside person to get answers. An answer from someone else, from a "professional," may seem more legitimate. Sometimes we're just lazy and want to be handed something on a platter. At other times, if we're in a jam and feeling all alone with it, there's a real sense of relief at having someone else see and recognize our predicament, to validate our belief that we're in a predicament. And using the process to help ourselves is scary. When we're clutching onto an issue with all our hopes and fears, it's difficult to let go, to surrender to the love with which we need to surround the question in order to let the Intuitive Heart guide us.

All of this is a long explanation to show you why I approach the Intuitive Heart method as a series of steps directed first at helping someone else. You can practice, understand and trust each part of the process before putting it all together, and you can learn to trust that it works, through validation by someone else, before practicing it to help yourself. By approaching the process this way, you can experience the growth of moving into a higher consciousness and of being willing to go through the experience of surrendering to the process.

Learning the process through first using it for someone else also helps you get past the illusion in which we all often live, that there is one objective, fixed answer. Edgar Cayce said that truth is a growing thing in the hearts and lives of individuals. His statement is a cousin to quantum physics' theory about the effect of the observer, the theory that reality is determined by the act of observation. Having other people give us answers lets us grab hold of something we see as fixed and "real," which certainly is comforting, but the answers they give still are more in their reality than in ours. When we go within ourselves and work, there is a very real sense of inescapable responsibility for growing our own truth. For many of us, this is too big a burden to carry at first, especially when we're confronting a crisis.

The secret to learning how to trust yourself, so that you can trust the process of relying upon intuition, especially in a crisis, is to not expect to make big leaps to the final answer. Find the smallest, first step of trust you can take.

Truth Is a Learning Process Growing into Beauty

"It is good to tell one's heart."   Chippewa Proverb

One other thing that you probably will realize very quickly is that the questions that we take to our intuition often do not lend themselves to simple yes-or-no answers. In living, we often deal with complex issues, and solutions are built on a whole series of questions and answers, many yes's and no's. The challenge is how to get inside that complexity, not to find a straightforward answer, which probably doesn't exist anyway, but to find a place to start. Even if you already know which mountain is worth climbing, you have to know where to place that first step, and you have to make decisions on where to put your feet all the way up that mountain, without knowing ahead of time all the details of the journey that will take you there.

Knowing all the steps beforehand is somewhat the

antithesis of the way life—and intuition—flows. In intuition, as in life, we have to be willing to allow the process to unfold.

I remember back to my efforts to stop smoking. I had run out of answers on how to quit. All I knew was that I was going to make a start and that I was determined to reach the goal. Everything in between was a huge question mark. By letting my intuition guide me, I saw where to take that first step, a step that ultimately led me on a successful journey:

> I began smoking at fourteen. By the time I was 18, I already was trying to quit. My only success at it, albeit a temporary one, was quitting for the pre-set time of a week when I was about nineteen. After that effort, the most I could go without a cigarette was a day. I tried everything. New Year's resolutions. Hypnosis. Groups. Prayers and promises to God. Rewards and punishments. Nothing worked. As the years went by and the smoking began to take a toll on my body, my motivation increased, but I still wasn't able to stop. In fact, it was only through working with the Intuitive Heart process for myself that I finally was able to put the cigarettes aside and not pick them up again.
>
> As I went through the process for myself, the first thing I got was that I no longer believed it was possible for me to quit and that the first thing I needed to do was to regain some confidence in my ability to even control my smoking. It came to me to simply count the cigarettes I smoked each day and not to smoke a cigarette without counting it first, that this would be, in some way, a significant step in regaining my confidence. So I began to count my cigarettes before I smoked them.

The help I got was not immediately the total answer to stopping, but over a period of two or three years, I did finish with the cigarettes and became smoke-free, with each step along the way being suggested by the intuitive process. I had been in a maze, trapped in this prison built by the cigarettes and my loss of confidence. By using my intuition to guide me, I gradually found a way out, the first way that ever had worked for me.

The point of this story is that we shouldn't assume that we should be able, no matter what the question, to get a complete and immediate solution when, in fact, we aren't always prepared to live out the answers that come. Change and growth often need to happen within us first. For myself, with the cigarettes, I had to accept that my body needed breaks, time out, for example. I had to learn that I couldn't just work straight through on projects but that I needed to get up, walk around, take a break. Cigarettes always had provided a substitute for those breaks, had suppressed the need for breaks. Through the Intuitive Heart discovery process, I came to understand that I had to give some time back to my body. These days, I walk for an hour every morning.

Another thing I had to learn was that I had to find a way to acknowledge and process my emotions. Cigarettes also were a way of suppressing my feelings. Since that realization, I have heard many people say they did fine in their efforts to stop smoking until they got angry or scared, and then they had a cigarette, that strong emotions would push them backwards. It was a realization and solution into which I had to grow.

The willingness to allow the process to unfold, I think, brings us back to something I mentioned a little earlier, that when we talk about intuition, it also sounds much of the time as if we are talking about matters of faith or spirituality. But what is intuition anyway? In my experience, it ultimately is a faith, a belief, a trust that you can draw upon yourself for that which you need, in harmony, in a greater truth, a greater love. Your lungs don't need to know the shape or rhythm of your next one thousand breaths in order for you to take the next one or to believe that the next one will come. Guided by the life force, our breath presents itself one breath at a time. The heart, too, takes one beat at a time, governed by this same life force. We don't have to attend consciously to each beat or try to make it happen to know that it will come.

I think another result of using this training method to develop or reinforce your intuitive abilities is that the training can carry you to a higher level of intuition, a higher level of connection with the whole. I think this explains why it's often difficult to use intuition to get ahead at the expense of others. Look at gambling, for example. Most gambling involves a zero-sum game, in which someone must lose in order for someone to win. Intuition doesn't seem to work well when someone else must pay the price of your getting ahead. It works best in situations that are win-win, such as working with others to create wealth, rather than just taking it away from someone else. This has a major bearing on the approach that I've taught you here, and it touches, too, on something that we'll look at more closely in Chapter 10, the spirituality of the Intuitive Heart. In the meantime, I'm going to give you still another technique to practice that can help build your confidence in using your intuition for yourself.

As you practice the method of the Intuitive Heart's path, you will find yourself more and more comfortable, skilled, and knowledgeable about what it means to follow this path with your heart, to allow your answers to come from within, to feel your connection with the outer world. You will find yourself more able to make adjustments, more filled with the inspiration, motivation, and ability to face the various circumstances your life brings. This is the path of the Intuitive Heart, and it is a path each of us can follow.

10

The Spirituality of the Intuitive Heart

"Blessed are the pure in heart: for they shall see God."

Matthew 5:8

*I*f you are trying to hit the target with your arrow, wouldn't you want to aim your bow, and very carefully? Not necessarily. Not if your real target is enlightenment. In his book, *Zen and the Art of Archery*, Eugene Herrigel tells of going to Japan to study Zen but of being unable to find a Japanese teacher who would take him on as a student. Finally, he heard about a renegade Zen teacher who was an archer. Herrigel approached this teacher with the hope of learning Zen through archery, and the teacher reluctantly agreed.

For a long time, Herrigel was allowed only to carry the

bow and arrows and to clean up after the teacher and do menial chores. Eventually, he progressed to being allowed to string the large and powerful bow, which was quite difficult and took a lot of learning. Finally, his teacher allowed him to notch an arrow and draw the bow, which required even more effortful learning.

One day, Herrigel arrived early and decided he would practice. He pulled back the bow, took aim at the target, and was ready to release the arrow, when he felt a whack to his face. His master had arrived, and he took away the bow and arrow from Herrigel in a startling and most unceremonious manner. Obviously upset, Herrigel's master shouted at him, "You fool! Anyone can learn to aim an arrow to hit the target—that's merely trick shooting!" The master dismissed Herrigel and told him to come back that night.

When Herrigel returned that evening as instructed, the master lit some candles and took him out into the archery field. He had Herrigel lift the target, move it far away, and place a candle beneath it. When Herrigel returned, he barely could make out the distant target, only dimly lit by the candle. His master instructed Herrigel to fasten a blindfold around the master's eyes. While Herrigel watched in rapt attention, his master asked for his bow, notched an arrow, and in one graceful sweeping motion, drew back the bow and released the arrow. He took off the blindfold and asked Herrigel to go look at the target. When Herrigel reached the target, he saw to his amazement that the arrow was in dead center!

When Herrigel brought back the arrow, his master instructed him, "You are here to learn Zen, not to learn how to aim your arrow at a target. To learn Zen, you must learn how to become one with the target. The arrow will do the rest by itself!"

Do You Want Intuition "Trickniques" or to Learn to Be Intuitive?

"It is not wisdom to be only wise,
And on the inward vision close the eyes,
But it is wisdom to believe the heart."
George Santayana, *O World, Thou Choosest Not*

The Intuitive Heart discovery process uses a mental process not just to gain insights, but also to develop a special quality of awareness. Like Herrigel's teacher, you are using an activity to develop an attitude of oneness, of deep, intuitive empathy. With this intuition training, you are learning how to become one with whatever it is you wish to understand. You gain insights along the way and can use the training process for guidance, yet you also are gaining something more.

There are other methods for getting answers from intuition. They may be shortcuts, quicker or easier to apply. They may, however, have no more to recommend them than the answers that they provide.

You could use a pendulum, for example, to get answers from the unconscious. You can make a pendulum by attaching a weight to a two-foot-long thread. Hold the thread so that the weight can swing freely. Now, you have a pendulum that you can use for determining inner truths. A pendulum's swing can detect very subtle "ideo-motor movements," which is a psychological term for unconscious body movements made in response to an idea. This sensitivity means that a pendulum can respond to the slightest movements of your hand. The hand, in turn, is influenced by thinking going on outside of your conscious awareness. Its movements can be used as way to "read" your subconscious mind. To the extent that your subconscious mind has access to information not available to consciousness, the pendulum makes an interesting tool for detecting that information.

You can ask the pendulum to indicate which direction of movement will indicate the answer, "yes," and which direction will indicate the answer, "no." Then you can pose yes/no questions and watch the pendulum's response. You can ask questions about what is in your best interests, for example, such as, "Shall I take up weight lifting for my health?" You can find out how your subconscious feels about this question.

Skilled hypnotists have found this method to be a very powerful way of bypassing the conscious censor to get at the truths hidden deep within and to formulate plans for treatment that the person will respond to positively.

Other practitioners use the pendulum like a psychic crystal ball. To the extent that the subconscious mind can be a channel of telepathic and clairvoyant information, or "non-local" information, to use a newer term popular with the scientifically minded, the pendulum method can provide answers to questions concerning matters outside the person's own sphere of knowledge. Presumably, the limits of devices such as the pendulum exist only in the skill of the questioning strategies used.

There are many other methods that work on a similar principle as the pendulum. The muscle-strength testing of kinesiology, which we discussed earlier, is one such example. The controversial Ouija board, using two people, is another example. What they all have in common is that they involve some form of "dissociation," or splitting, separating the conscious mind from the process, so that the subconscious mind can produce information directly.

Using these "trickniques" requires some skill development, and they can provide useful information. But they teach neither intuition development nor any personal development resembling even the learning of empathy or oneness, much less spirituality. In some ways, that deficiency is their merit, for these methodologies go directly to the specific task at hand—gathering information. Learning intuition, especially learning to be on familiar terms with your Intuitive Heart, requires something more, and gives something more in return. Instead of just gathering information, you are accessing wisdom.

We know that we want our intuitive process to be clear of "ego," but the kind of bypassing of the ego that these trickniques provide is really a shortcut that shortchanges us. When we bypass the ego, it is like sending it out of the room every time we want to get an answer. It's out of the way, certainly, but then it never learns how to sit quietly and open itself to intuition. The Intuitive Heart discovery process invites the ego to participate and trains it to relax and accept what comes. This method trains the ego to identify with an ideal that takes it beyond itself. In this way, we don't simply learn how to tap the subconscious mind. We also teach the whole person how to come into harmony with larger truths.

Edgar Cayce had highly developed intuitive gifts. From an intuitive state of awareness, he gave discourses on several subjects, one of which was the development of intuition, including psychic abilities. Like Herrigel's Zen master, Cayce took a larger view, saying that focusing on learning how to make telepathic "hits" (as in ESP tests) really misses the point. The real point, Cayce said, is learning how to make meaningful connections with others for the purpose of being helpful. In doing this, he explained, one can learn the true nature of intuitive and psychic gifts and the possibilities inherent in them.

Spirituality Is in the Oneness

"For the human heart is the mirror
Of the things that are near and far;
Like the wave that reflects in its bosom
The flower and the distant star."

Alice Cary, *The Time to Be*

When Aldous Huxley researched the world's religions to identify common elements, he wrote *The Perennial Philosophy* to share what he had learned. The essence of the world's spiritual teaching could be summarized, he believed, in this simple declaration: "Thou Art That!" In other words, the world out there and the you inside are one and the same. This basic spiritual axiom of oneness has received scientific confirmation in modern physics, which has found that the essence of matter is nonphysical, and this nonphysical essence is of one piece and interconnected. In his book, *The Medium, The Mystic and The Physicist,* Lawrence LeShan showed how the perceptions of these three groups essentially are identical. The essence of universal spirituality has received scientific backing!

It's one thing to understand the concept of oneness, as a scientific theory. It's another thing to live it. It's one thing to understand the scientific theory that allows for and explains the possibility of intuition. It's another to have the direct experience, the intuition, of oneness.

Intuition training does involve some work in the experience of oneness. In my research on intuition training methods, I've found that the methods all share certain characteristics. The first is that they teach you that you must trust. Through whatever method is involved, you are learning to trust your intuition, to trust in your experience, to go with whatever comes to you, to accept the flow of your mind or mental imagery or whatever it is that particular method uses. Learning to accept, to trust, is a precondition for experiencing oneness. The consciousness of oneness says "yes" to experiences, not "no," or "I'll think about it." Some methods get you to think about trusting, while other methods get you actually to "do" trust.

As you have seen in our training of your Intuitive Heart, the breath is a natural teacher about trust as well as about the intuitive process. I like using the breath as a teacher because it takes you into the mystery of what flow is about, into the larger harmony of things. You learn about trust in the personal sense of releasing and accepting, but you also learn about trust in the larger sense of accepting the rightness of the harmonious flow of life. You can begin to experience trust as an acceptance, even an embrace, of the sense of oneness with all life. It is one of the gifts of the breath.

One thing I've learned about myself is that, as much as I would like to have all my actions and thoughts governed by the highest principles, my mind has a will of its own, leading me into a lot of fretting and worrying. But as I practice the Intuitive Heart discovery process, I find that my fretting and worrying are no longer so necessary, that I can get the helpful guidance I need. In getting that guidance, I also get, as a bonus, some relaxation and a direct, reassuring, loving reminder that I'm okay and a part of an okay world.

In developing the Intuitive Heart method, one thing on which I have focused is the naturalness of it, the idea that we all have a natural ability to be intuitive and to connect with that ability and its inherent oneness. Interconnectedness exists, whether we are aware of it or not, and I've structured the Intuitive Heart method to demonstrate how it is possible to introduce your own natural way of being to this creative existence. It is a way of opening the door into this oneness and harmony, perhaps even a way of reintroducing us to "Paradise," where people could live in harmony through living intuitively.

Most intuition training methods also include a technique to get the participant into a facilitative state of higher awareness. Some use relaxation; some use alpha brain-wave methods. Others use affirmations or prayers. But there is a difference between a state of higher awareness and a state of flow. Higher awareness is not necessarily oneness.

The major discovery of the Intuitive Heart is that we have a natural way of getting into higher consciousness *and* the oneness of flow. That way is through love, and it happens naturally when our heart goes out to someone and we care to help them. At the moment of our heart's reaching out, we build an intuitive bridge.

We want to take advantage of this natural human response and enlist it in the service of learning the Intuitive Heart process. By using it and experiencing how well it works in helping another person, we can develop confidence in this meditation on the heart, on love and gratitude in the heart, on the energy that comes through the heart. We can step out of our own way, surrender to it, and take an important step onto the path of the highest state of consciousness, to a place where we are coming from love.

The Spirituality Is in Experiencing the Connection

"The workings of the human heart are the profoundest mystery of the universe. One moment they make us despair of our kind, and the next we see in them the reflection of the divine image."
                                                    Charles W. Chestnut

In your study of the Intuitive Heart discovery process

and my suggestions for practice, if you've ever asked yourself if it's really worth the effort—getting into flow, into gratefulness, into the heart connection when there might be quicker ways to try to get the answers you need—you're not alone, I'm sure. I'm also just as sure that it is worth the effort. Besides the benefits of spiritual development, there's a payoff in enjoyment and in the experience of empathy with other persons, life forms and aesthetic experiences.

Something that people often tell me when they practice the Intuitive Heart method with another person is how close they come to feel to that person. Two strangers can leave their encounter feeling as if they have known each other for a long time.

They also often use the word "spiritual" to describe their experience because it deals with feeling connected at the level of essences. Many of us give lip service to the idea that we all are one and interconnected, but it's not something we actually experience very often in most parts of our lives because our ordinary physical senses tell us otherwise. With our eyes, we can see that we are separate. We also can hear, feel, and smell the presence of another person as a being outside ourselves. When one person eats an apple, we can see that the apple is not there for us to eat. But through the Intuitive Heart discovery process, we can, figuratively speaking, share with them the experience of eating that apple. We can draw upon memories that will help us relate to that person. In the same way, when that person is going through a challenge, we can come up with something that helps us establish that connection, that reminds us of lessons we have learned and that joins us together.

In researching and reviewing the various approaches to spirituality, it seems that the essence is that it is something that we *experience* rather than simply *believe*. What we experience, primarily, is a sense of connection. We feel connected to life, sense that everything in life is connected, and feel connected to something "higher" or "greater" or "beyond" ourselves. This sense of connection is something beyond what meets the eyes: It is something more than a physical sensation, and it involves something higher than immediate concerns. It is a connection with the *essence* or *spirit* of life.

We have seen how the breath meditation and the making of the heart connection express the meaning of the Hawaiian approach to spirituality, "Aloha!" Their familiar greeting, "Let's share the sacred breath given us by the Creator," is a friendly invitation to spirituality. Here, again, spirituality lives in the sense of connection.

The Intuitive Heart Expresses the Spirituality of Shamanism

"As he thinketh in his heart, so is he."   Proverbs 23:7

Another dimension of this sense of spiritual connection can be found in shamanism. There is a great deal of interest these days in shamanism—dating back to the books by Carlos Casteneda—and it goes beyond the ethnic artifacts and into shamanism's practices. Shamans—people who are combinations of healers, teachers, artists, and magicians—usually are initiated into their training through an illness or other extreme difficulty. Traditionally, they have viewed their challenge as coming from the Creative Spirit, asking them to change themselves, or even to transform their whole way of being in order to achieve healing.

Initiated shamans have been called "wounded healers." They have been wounded by the gods, either physically, mentally, or emotionally, and they find healing from within themselves. This inward orientation is the basis of the healing gifts they share with others. It is how they earned their "medicine." Shamans approach those people they would help with the attitude that everything happens for a purpose, including illness. With the patient, they search for the illness's purpose, try to help the illness fulfill that purpose, and find healing in that way.

The shaman's method of practice often involves using an altered state of consciousness. They go within themselves, on a "soul's journey" in search of the soul of the patient or the patient's guardian spirit, in order to work out a plan for healing. They return from this journey with a story to tell the patient and a plan of action.

The essence of the Intuitive Heart discovery process is very much like the essence of shamanism. Using this process, we help another by going inside ourselves. We enter the altered state of consciousness of love and gratitude. We invite a memory to come to us, a "familiar" (which is a shamanic term for a spirit guide), the "spirit" of prior experience that comes into our place of inner meditation. We ask what it has to teach us, and we share that teaching with the person we are trying to help.

The wisdom that we share comes from our own wounds, our own learning from experience. We share of our own learning, providing healing and help through, you might say, the distilled juices of our own struggles. The spirit that comes to us through the memory activates the spirit in the other person. They experience this spirit in the recognition of a truth that they can see, of an emotional response to our sharing. Spirit speaks to spirit, as heart speaks to heart.

Another resemblance between shamanism and the Intuitive Heart discovery process is in making connections with the invisible realm of "spirits." Shamans are in communication with spiritual influences, which they experience as living beings, and which we generally might interpret as the living spirit in all things. The Intuitive Heart, with its gifted imagination, can make special connections with plants, animals, and environments just as easily as with people. The love-centered approach of the Intuitive Heart also provides a protective framework for this kind of exploration.

Love Has No Need for Power

"Two chambers hath the heart.
There dwelling, Live Joy and Pain apart."
                                    Hermann Neumann, *Das Herz*

The Intuitive Heart can take us to a sacred place, this loving point of connection with the whole, in just a relatively few minutes, instead of the lifetime that many of us spend struggling to find where we fit. It reminds us that we can trust in the flow of life, that we can trust inspiration at both the mundane level of the breath in our lungs and at the spiritual level of the thoughts and feelings that come to us. In those same few minutes, it can teach us to experience gratitude and joy in the flow of connection with the whole, bringing with it a memory or image that we can share with another or use to help ourselves. In these few moments, we can create a sacred circle of having our innermost being embraced by the outer world.

With the Intuitive Heart discovery process, I have put together what I have learned about intuition into a training exercise. But as I have shared this method with people and practiced it for myself, I have come to recognize that it is much more than an exercise or method; it also is a path. Intuition and the Intuitive Heart method are a form of meditation. Like any good meditation, it is one that you can practice any time, whenever you feel the need for guidance on a question or concern.

The stresses in our lives are a signal, a signal that we are working against a resistance, that we have fallen out of the world's harmony. I see this echoed now in the many books whose themes are the silver linings behind clouds, how people struggle with adversity and then learn to turn it to their advantage. Perhaps this is a result of the rapid, stressful changes in our world that shock our expectations by shaking up the status quo. The Intuitive Heart can help us to reenter the world's harmony, to sing in harmony again by getting us back into tune. This search for harmony with our world brings us yet again to the path of spirituality.

So the Intuitive Heart is of the spirit, not just a technique. It is a way of approaching the world. It reflects some very ancient truths and wisdom about sharing your spirit, giving testimony to another person's spirit and, in that sense, it is not new. I think, however, that the method I've developed to connect with the Intuitive Heart does offer something new by simplifying a process into terms we all can understand. It allows us to make up our own minds and to see our own learning. It helps us to be honest in our dealings with ourselves and others. It helps us to find an alternative to the need for power.

Power—over others, over our environment, over our lives—is a real concern for many of us in today's world. We struggle for power, and we end up struggling with one another and with nature. Is there no other way?

My own story is one of learning that love has no need for power. In my first book, *Getting Help from Dreams*, I told my personal story of shamanic initiation, how I became a wounded healer. It was through alcoholism. I wanted to have the power of creativity, but I didn't want to make any sacrifices to have it. I wanted to own it, to have it for my own use. I found the spirit in the bottle. I could pull it out when I wanted, and it freed me to create in new ways. But it also tricked me. I learned that it had power over me. I tried to conquer it, but I couldn't. When I accepted that I was helpless against it and surrendered to a higher power, I had learned my first lesson. But later, an even bigger lesson came my way. What I called a higher *power* wasn't really power at all (at least not in the way we usually think of that word), but *love*.

Before the idea that "love is letting go of fear" was popularized by *A Course in Miracles* and before spirituality became the theme song of the recovery movement, it came to me in a meditation that "love has no need for power." I also noticed that I did not like that thought.

I reflected upon what I had learned from alcoholism. One thing the experience had taught me was that alcoholics often have a power complex because they feel very weak in some way and want to break through to a level of experience that will overcome that weakness. They are attracted to alcohol as a way to try to achieve that breakthrough, to have power over it, and are undone by the alcohol at the same time. Much of current alcoholism recovery work involves surrendering to a higher power rather than trying to achieve personal power. It came to me in the meditation that the concept of a higher power is a transitional concept to wean us away from even thinking in terms of power, to move us towards coming from a place of love. The reason I didn't like that thought was that I was not very trusting of love. It made me feel too vulnerable. I couldn't be in control.

Soon, I discovered the breath meditation. It was a simple but soothing place for me to explore feelings of control, trust, letting go, openness, and vulnerability. It was a laboratory for my own growth. It is the place from which the Intuitive Heart comes as well, a place where power is unnecessary because we already are part of everything. It helped me prepare myself for further lessons that would come my way.

One of my hardest lessons had to do with having power over pain and suffering. I hesitate to write of this topic, but I must, so I "knock on wood," lest any of this be taken as pride of accomplishment, when in reality, I'm but a young student of the Intuitive Heart path.

The heart is a paradox: It can know both pain and joy. The lesson with which I struggled in my own practice of the Intuitive Heart method was the one carried within another one of those wonderful heart metaphors: Open up your heart. The receptivity that is involved in acceptance of the Intuitive Heart's messages also lowers the shields we erect against suffering. In working with our intuitive abilities, we voluntarily accept the lowering of those shields in order to enter flow and its connections, even though we then will be undefended against hurt. Both as a child and as a younger man, I could not make that trade. It has taken many years for me to recognize that closing myself off from pain is far more deadening and, ultimately and ironically, far more painful, than to be open to the "mixed" blessings of intuition's connections.

A former teacher of mine told me that one of the difficult lessons she has learned in her long life is that everything has a purpose, that even the bad things are good things in disguise, showing us how to grow. In working with the Intuitive Heart discovery process, I have found the strength and confidence to deal with old wounds, to cry old, unshed tears. The Intuitive Heart lets us learn these lessons in little steps at first, teaching us by bringing up a memory in which we find some teaching for ourselves and then using it to connect with another.

Gradually, we come to understand the truth of what Victor Frankl said, that we can endure almost any pain as long as we can understand the "why." And when we then begin to apply the Intuitive Heart discovery process for ourselves, we find in it teachings that help us deal with our own situation. We find the meaning, the "why", in our own lives.

There is a flip side as well. The Intuitive Heart not only takes us on a journey through our own hearts, with all its memories and, sometimes, its pain, but it also takes us on a journey to oneness and joy. By learning to trust our intuition, which is trusting the essence, the most real parts of ourselves, we can allow our lives to flow upward and outward, into the inherent harmony of all life. It is a journey well worth taking. May you discover your own Intuitive Heart. It is a heart we all share.

About the Authors

Henry Reed divides his time between being a goat rancher and being an independent scholar of psychology, involved in writing, teaching, consulting, research, and counseling.

He received his Ph.D. from U.C.L.A. and was Assistant Professor of Psychology at Princeton University and Professor of Transpersonal Studies at Atlantic University. He has authored several popular books and professional articles and produced several instructional videos.

He has been called the "father of the dreamwork movement" because of his creation of *Sundance: The Community Dream Journal,* that helped spark the national dreamwork movement.

He has a private counseling practice in Mouth of Wilson, Virginia, specializing in intensive, transformational work, centered in dreams, energetic healing, and creativity; is the founder of Creative Spirit Studios; is involved in consulting on a three-hour series on dreams for the Discovery Channel; and is creating an "Intuitive Heart Discovery Group" network around the country, training people to become Intuitive Heart™ practitioners.

You can reach Henry at 3777 Fox Creek Road, Mouth of Wilson, VA 23451; 1-800-398-1370; e-mail: Starbuck@ls.net; Web site: www.creativespirit.net.

Brenda English is a longtime student of Henry Reed's Intuitive Heart discovery process. She has worked as a newspaper reporter in Florida and Michigan, as a hospital publications manager in the Washington, D.C., area, and is the author of three books in the Sutton McPhee Mystery Series.

A.R.E. PRESS

The A.R.E. Press publishes books, videos, and audiotapes meant to improve the quality of our readers' lives—personally, professionally, and spiritually. We hope our products support your endeavors to realize your career potential, to enhance your relationships, to improve your health, and to encourage you to make the changes necessary to live a loving, joyful, and fulfilling life.

For more information or to receive a free catalog, call:

1-800-723-1112

Or write:

A.R.E. Press
215 67th Street
Virginia Beach, VA 23451-2061

DISCOVER HOW THE EDGAR CAYCE MATERIAL CAN HELP YOU!

The Association for Research and Enlightenment, Inc. (A.R.E.®), was founded in 1931 by Edgar Cayce. Its international headquarters are in Virginia Beach, Virginia, where thousands of visitors come year round. Many more are helped and inspired by A.R.E.'s local activities in their own hometowns or by contact via mail (and now the Internet!) with A.R.E. headquarters.

People from all walks of life, all around the world, have discovered meaningful and life-transforming insights in the A.R.E. programs and materials, which focus on such areas as personal spirituality, holistic health, dreams, family life, finding your best vocation, reincarnation, ESP, meditation, and soul growth in small-group settings. Call us today at our toll-free number:

1-800-333-4499

or

Explore our electronic visitors center on the
Internet: **http://www.edgarcayce.org.**

We'll be happy to tell you more about how the work of the A.R.E. can help you!

A.R.E.
215 67th Street
Virginia Beach, VA 23451-2061